RESPECT
TRUMPS
HARMONY

RESPECT

TRUMPS

HARMONY

WHY BEING LIKED IS OVERRATED AND CONSTRUCTIVE CONFLICT GETS RESULTS

RACHAEL ROBERTSON

WILEY

First published in 2020 by John Wiley & Sons Australia, Ltd
42 McDougall St, Milton Qld 4064

Office also in Melbourne

Typeset in 10.5pt/13.5pt Palatino LT Std Light

© John Wiley & Sons Australia, Ltd 2020

The moral rights of the author have been asserted

ISBN: 978-0-730-38383-3

 A catalogue record for this book is available from the National Library of Australia

Cover design by Wiley
Cover image © Orla / Getty Images

10 9 8 7 6 5 4 3 2 1

Disclaimer
The material in this publication is of the nature of general comment only, and does not represent professional advice. It is not intended to provide specific guidance for particular circumstances and it should not be relied on as the basis for any decision to take action or not take action on any matter which it covers. Readers should obtain professional advice where appropriate, before making any such decision. To the maximum extent permitted by law, the author and publisher disclaim all responsibility and liability to any person, arising directly or indirectly from any person taking or not taking action based on the information in this publication.

CONTENTS

ABOUT THE AUTHOR

Rachael Robertson is one of the most popular and in-demand keynote speakers in the world today. She presents internationally at over 80 events a year, drawing on her own experience to provide audiences with practical tools to build resilient, collaborative and high-performing teams.

Rachael speaks and writes from first-hand knowledge. She has experienced both extremes of opportunity and challenge. She led an Antarctic expedition, was one of Victoria's youngest Chief Rangers and was a key part of the response team during Victoria's Black Saturday bushfire tragedy. She holds an MBA from Melbourne Business School, one of only two globally recognised post-graduate business schools in Australia, and blends her practical insights with contemporary leadership theory.

Using a combination of real life case-studies, extensive research and hilarious anecdotes from her year spent working in Antarctica, Rachael presents memorable and proven leadership tools, and has worked extensively throughout Australia, New Zealand, Asia, Europe and the United States sharing her iconic tools: No Triangles and the Bacon War. Her approach is down-to-earth and engaging, there is no management-speak and no jargon—just practical, proven and easy-to-implement tools for building leadership and teamwork.

The best-selling author of *Leading on the Edge*, Rachael is now a full-time professional speaker, commentator and author. She is an Ambassador for R U OK? and as an internationally acclaimed leadership expert she knows her way around an airport. Rachael honestly and candidly acknowledges most of her career choices were made because she believes 'it's better to regret what you did, than regret what you didn't do.'

She lives in Melbourne, Australia, with her husband Ric, and her son Louis, and can be found most Saturdays in winter standing in the cold at an AFL match somewhere.

ACKNOWLEDGEMENTS

This book has been 15 years in the making. It would not have been possible without the generosity and kindness of so many people. I am grateful for your support and willingness to offer your hearts and minds, and for trusting me to share your stories and experiences.

Firstly, and most importantly, a big thank you to my extraordinary husband and partner in crime, Ric. Thank you for your unwavering belief in me. I could not do what I do, and share what I've learned, without you. I wouldn't want to either. Your encouragement drives me, and knowing you are on the end of a phone as I wait out yet another flight delay reminds me that what truly matters is love and laughter! You are my world.

To Louie, thank you for choosing me to be your mum. I think you're the best and you make me laugh. Thank you for so generously staying quiet, playing on the iPad while I finished writing this book during the school holidays. I'm so proud of you.

Doug, Julian, Anthony and Georgina, thank you for all your love and encouragement over many years. Watching you grow into loving, warm, hilarious and (just quietly) strikingly good-looking adults is one of my greatest joys. Keep flying the Team Lamont flag with such strength and grace. I see so much of Nanna Spanna in all of you, and your love of family, travel and life is her gift to you.

To my wonderful family, Mum, Dad, Ben, Jane, Sam, Tim and Aunty Pammy, thanks for simply being there, especially when I can't be. Thanks for holding the fort and feeding pets and watering gardens, sometimes at very short notice. I couldn't do it without you.

Martine, Tanya and Dallas, where do I start? Usually, it's with a wine! Thanks for the debriefs, the laugh-till-we-cry times, and for keeping my head above water as that monster wave called life comes crashing in. I love doing life with you girls.

Thanks to the amazing team at Wiley, especially Lucy Raymond and my editor Jem Bates. Your patience, advice and insights are much appreciated. You're the best in the business for a reason.

To the more than 1500 organisations who have invited me to present at your conferences and events, I am sincerely humble and grateful. Thank you for trusting me with your teams. I put everything I have into every presentation. I'm often asked if I still get nervous. The answer is 'yes'. Not because of my content—I know that backwards—but because I truly care that what I am presenting resonates and inspires. I get nervous because I am invested, and the day I don't get nervous is the day I walk away.

Lastly, to every person who answered my call for help and completed a survey or offered their time for a follow-up phone interview, a huge thank you. Your input was invaluable. Thank you for trusting me with your stories, and for being candid and generous with your time. I will be forever grateful that you joined me on this quest to build a world with a bit more respect.

Because *respect trumps harmony,* every time.

INTRODUCTION

In 2005 I was chosen to lead an expedition to Davis Station, Antarctica. I was the second woman to lead the station, and one of the youngest ever leaders there. It was an extraordinary experience that tested me in ways I could never have predicted.

I had no input into the selection of my 17 team members. As is the norm in most jobs, I was presented with a disparate group of people I had never met. Somehow I had to turn this random assortment of diverse individuals into a high-performing team—because in Antarctica our lives would depend on our teamwork.

At our first 'get to know you' barbecue in Hobart I found myself chatting with two of the team about cold weather. One of them said: 'I was just in Alaska; it was so cold that when you stood in a puddle the water turned to ice under your feet. It must have been at least minus 21 degrees.' The other replied: 'Well, water freezes at zero, so it must have been at least zero, not at least minus 21 degrees.'

Oh dear. That exchange set me on a journey, which continues to this day, to find a way to build a team that focuses on raising and dealing with issues professionally, and respectfully. My two biggest concerns in Antarctica were of someone exploding with anger or someone spiralling into depression, because I didn't feel I had the resources to handle either of those situations. So instead I set about developing a culture that would encourage us all to speak up, speak out, raise issues, deal with them and move on.

After the expedition I started presenting at conferences and events what I had learned and the tools I had used at Davis Station. At the start it was only an event here and there, but then things just took off. I now present at over 100 events a year around the world. And while I have refined the content over time in response to changing perspectives and current hot topics, the fundamental tools I use remain the same.

Quite soon I found there were so many common questions coming up at every keynote presentation that I decided to write a book to address those questions. That book, *Leading on the Edge*, achieved bestseller status in six weeks and has been optioned to Netflix. It is still selling incredibly well—not, I hasten to say, because it's particularly mind-blowing, but because the insights it offers are practical, real and, most importantly, proven. It's not the *what* or *why*—it's the *how*.

Over the past 15 years I have had countless messages from people sharing their stories of implementing my leadership and teamwork tools. Without exception, every one of them has recounted how the tools have helped them. In some cases, it may have been no more than a tweak here or there, but for others it has had a significant impact on their work, and consequently their life.

It intrigued me that across the 1500 teams I had worked with— from corporations and the public sector, not-for-profits, schools, volunteer groups—the challenges were much the same.

We all agree that diversity is great, and the evidence is unequivocal that it has an impact on the bottom line. In the public sector and volunteer organisations it is vital that staff represent the community they serve. But as our teams get more and more diverse we won't always see eye to eye, we won't always agree on things. So how do we create a culture where that's okay? How do we encourage constructive debate and robust discussion? How do we address issues directly and professionally?

Every team wants three things—performance, respect and harmony. Of course every business strives especially for results, but this is not the focus of this book. Rather, it is about achieving the balance between respect and harmony that makes great results possible.

To research this book, we surveyed almost 200 teams who had already implemented these tools, and conducted follow-up interviews with 30 people to gather further insights. I wanted to know what worked for them and what didn't. And what changed as a result of implementing the tools.

I identify the three tools that lie at the core of the leadership practice I prescribe as follows:

- **No triangles**—a tool to put an end to gossip, improve accountability and the quality of feedback, and drive innovation

- **The bacon war**—a gentle circuit-breaker for calling out dysfunctional behaviour

- **Lead without a title**—an approach to developing personal leadership in your team, so responsibility and initiative are shared.

These tools are the three pillars that hold up the *respect trumps harmony* culture.

In gathering the 15 years of research, case studies and feedback that inform this book I made the decision to broaden the scope from a purely business setting, because I believe the same principles apply in sporting clubs, volunteer groups and even within families. So feel free to apply these ideas across any team relevant to you.

What do I mean when I talk about harmony?

A quick internet search will tell you all you need to know about the importance of harmony as a pathway to a high-performing team. While researching this book I spent a couple of days digging through the first ten pages of a Google search on 'harmonious teams'. With just one exception (an entry that referenced me), all spoke of the critical need for team harmony. Whether at work or in a volunteer or sports team, the value of liking and getting on with those around us seems self-evident.

Ultimately, team performance is about results. Did we deliver this project on time and within budget, and in a way that delighted the customer? Did our sporting team finish the year two or three rungs higher than last year? Results are what matter, particularly when dollars and reputations are at stake—and sometimes when enough resources are in play, a carefully selected team of high-performing individuals can clinch these results. Most of us don't get to choose our teams, though. We get who or what we're given, yet are still expected to deliver the required outcomes.

Cohesion is an important part of any team, but do you achieve it simply by liking one another? Or does it result from a combination of heading towards a common goal, respecting what each other brings to the table *and* focusing on results? I think the latter, clearly. Hence the central idea of this book.

I will argue that it's totally okay if we don't *like* each other, but to get results we do need to *respect* each other. This is the main idea we're going to unpack over the next 140 or so pages. We will share some stories of course, and some theories or models as you'd expect, but more importantly we will explore some practical ways to identify and solve common problems that crop up in teams at work, in social groups and within families.

No one can seriously expect a team of individually selected people chosen solely for their unique set of skills and capabilities to all warm to each other and agree on everything. We all want to enjoy going to work, because doing a job that isn't any fun is really hard. But it's unrealistic to think we will always be best friends with the people we work with. Similarly, there will be people in the community, and possibly even in our families, who really push our buttons. We don't always have to get along, but we must always act with respect.

The three tools described in this book can be used in any team setting—business, community or family. As the results show, implementing these tools has an immediate and positive impact on teams of all kinds. It ensures people feel valued and heard and builds a sense of common purpose. It helps people speak up when they aren't travelling so well, or when they have a great idea they'd like to share.

We don't all have to love each other, in fact we don't even have to like each other, but we do need to treat each other with respect. Because *respect trumps harmony*, every time.

One of the toughest workplaces on the planet

In 2005 I had a unique opportunity to leave behind a comfortable senior leadership role in a safe environment, surrounded by people I knew, liked and respected, and head off to the wilds of Antarctica for a year. Those of you who have read my first book, *Leading on the Edge*, will know that, as much as it was an experiment, it was no accident. I had been working on my leadership skills for a decade and was itching to get my hands on a leadership role of truly epic proportions.

A lot of what I encountered down there on the ice was expected—it was in the brochure. Yes, it was a cold, dry and harsh environment that taxed you physically and mentally. Yes, we developed strong relationships over the 18 months we were together and no, I wouldn't do it again.

It was the unexpected things that stretched me, and there were plenty of those. In any role (be it a work, family or social setting) we bring a base set of skills and knowledge that we are confident in, and expected events help us shape and refine these, and grow new ones.

My first unexpected event was that I was to be 'given' a team. I would play no part in identifying, selecting, recruiting or onboarding the 120 people who would join my expedition over the summer, or the 17 who would stay behind with me over the long nine months of the cold, dark winter as we prepared for the next batch of expeditioners the following year. What would this teach me? What could I learn from the opportunity to shape a disparate set of individuals into a high-performing team?

I started looking at who we had and met each person individually, looking for a common thread. I failed. Miserably. Most of us had little or nothing in common, other than having all made the seemingly crazy decision to live and work in Antarctica for a season.

Antarctica … let me set the scene:

- **Cold.** It's the coldest continent on the planet, with temperatures plummeting to minus 80 degrees.

- **Dry.** Most of Antarctica hasn't seen rain since before the last ice age.

- **Windy.** Cold air sweeps down the mountains of Antarctica at anything from 100 km/h to over 300 km/h in some places.

- **Desolate.** There's not a single tree on the entire continent.

- **Dangerous.** Hidden snow bridges over deep ice crevasses are everywhere, and exposure in these conditions can be lethal.

This was to be our workplace and our home.

Under the terms of the Antarctic Treaty, countries with a 'stake' in the continent have established their own research stations where they conduct scientific experiments ranging from climate monitoring and seismology to meteorology (meteors are most commonly found in Antarctica because they stand out against the white ice and snow). Usually these bases are situated in coastal areas where they are easiest to resupply.

Australia maintains three such stations: Mawson, Casey and Davis. I was assigned to Davis Station, the largest and most southerly of the three, which carries the biggest scientific load over summer.

So, I wondered, what happens when you put a bunch of strangers in extremely cramped living quarters in an inherently dangerous workplace environment for a year with minimal contact with the outside world? How will you bring them together as a team? How will you stop them from killing each other over petty grievances? How will you keep them safe, both physically and psychologically, when it's too dangerous even to step outside for a short walk to 'blow off steam'?

I sat down and made a list of challenges that I suspected I and my fellow expeditioners might face over the coming year.

PHYSICAL HEALTH AND SAFETY

Antarctica is one of the most inherently dangerous workplaces on the planet, the harsh environment exacerbated by:

- limited medical facilities—one doctor, a small operating theatre and the IT guy doubling up as a theatre nurse

- the extreme difficulty of evacuation in an emergency—through the long winter months between March and November, help could be months away

- the inescapable fact that if anyone is unable to work through sickness or injury, other team members will have to pick up the load. The work still has to be done, even down to mundane chores such as housekeeping and cleaning.

MENTAL HEALTH AND SAFETY

We would be living on top of each other, confined to a handful of cramped buildings, for an entire year. How would we deal with this restrictive environment, including:

- the lack of privacy—everyone would know everything; if you were having a bad day the team would know

- homesickness, which no amount of phoning home can assuage

- the lack of normal support structures—no family, community or church get-togethers, no sports meets; you can't even take the dog for a walk

- comprehensive change in relation to diet, technology, job design, recreation and environment

- greatly reduced personal choices and options. (Feel like pasta for dinner tonight? You're out of luck, the chef has cooked roast chicken.)

- lack of intimacy—for most of us it's an entire year without so much as a hug.

THE WORK ITSELF

For many people, joining the Australian Public Service, and grappling with the mountain of policies and procedures you must follow when you are funded by the taxpayer, requires an adjustment. Add to this:

- Many expeditioners, in particular the tradespeople, had only ever been self-employed and answerable to no one except their customers.

- Living in a different time zone, we were operating several hours behind head office, which meant sometimes any answer to our questions would not arrive until the next day.

- Head office could not know in any real sense what was happening on the ground.

- Multiple reporting lines meant that while I was leader on station, my team were accountable to heads of science programs in universities, engineering teams, communications teams and so on. It was a complex matrix of responsibilities and reporting.

As their leader, I knew I would face an additional set of challenges. I would always be on duty. Even on a Sunday (typically a day off during winter) I would still be at work, and still be the leader. As with all leadership roles, I was under intense scrutiny and I knew that every decision, no matter how trivial, would be dissected and critiqued.

Then there was the additional challenge of performance management. How would I manage poor performance without any sanctions, or acknowledge excellence without any tangible rewards?

Throw all this together and it became a formidable list of challenges. And through it all we needed to deliver the science projects, run the station over both summer and winter, maintain the infrastructure and prepare for the next batch of expeditioners.

With a bunch of random strangers.

In a nutshell

- People are stressed by very different things. What might be simple for one person might completely derail someone else. Knowing and accepting that stressors are personal helps build empathy.
- The impact of change tends to be cumulative. For example, one change, such as a change to their start time, might not affect someone too much, but add a restructure, talk of an office relocation and chatter about a merger, and the cumulative impact can have be massive.

Diversity is being invited to the party; inclusion is being asked to dance

I've mentioned that the only thing the members of our expedition team had in common was that we had all made the quite radical decision to live in Antarctica. I hadn't expected this. I had assumed, incorrectly, that we would have similar backgrounds, or be around the same age, or share a similar passion for adventure. This was not the case, but it took me a while to discover it.

Looking through my team photos, I was first struck by how similar we were. All white, mostly men. Finding common threads of shared values, experiences and stories should be easy, I thought. But it turned out that the more I got to know them, the more diverse I realised we were.

I am all for diversity and being proactive about it. The business case for diversity is rock solid. There is a ton of research showing how diverse teams, when this diversity is utilised well, make better decisions and are more innovative. There are also dozens of case studies showing how teams have become ineffective because they couldn't create an environment that made the most of their team members' differences.

Diversity goes so much deeper than what you can see, of course. It goes far beyond race, age and gender. On these counts you would look at my team and think we were close to 90 per cent homogeneous.

Which was far from the truth, though I wouldn't discover this for a long time, when I had got to know and understand each individual. In my small team of expeditioners who were to remain behind through the winter—in addition to race, gender and age—this diversity was manifested in:

- education levels (from trade school through to multiple postgraduate degrees)
- thinking styles (from logical and rational to emotional and intuitive)
- conflict handling (from the hot-headed through to those who would internalise discord and stew)
- professional background and work experience
- generation (Millennials through to baby boomers)
- relationship status (single, couple, with or without a family, divorced or widowed)
- family responsibilities (with children or other dependants, such as elderly parents or a relative with special needs)
- sexual orientation

- introvert versus extrovert

- socioeconomic background

- life experience (some had only ever lived in rural or regional Australia, while others had lived overseas for long stints and moved regularly)

- ethnic background (first-generation through to fifth-generation Australian)

- Antarctic experience (first-timers through to veterans who have made multiple trips)

- appetite for risk and the unknown (embracing or resisting change).

If you drill down beneath what's visible and obvious in your team, what other forms of diversity might you find? This is an interesting and worthwhile exercise for all teams. The more you know about team members, the better you will be able to understand their behaviours and what drives them.

While demographic diversity is often more visible and apparent, cognitive diversity can be more challenging, but also more rewarding. Cognitive diversity relates to different ways of thinking, viewpoints and skill sets. It also includes cultural intelligence — that is, the ability to thrive in different cultural settings.

A priority when working in Antarctica is the need to collaborate with representatives of other nations. As in multicultural communities, or multinational companies, the ability to empathise and understand cultural differences is crucial. If you're in doubt or unsure, just ask. It is better to show respect by asking if you don't understand a cultural reference, response or ritual, rather than merely pretending you're across it to maintain superficial harmony, because it shows you actually care.

When I worked with Bunnings I came across a team leader held in high regard by one particular team member. Why? Because he had taken the time to learn the correct pronunciation of her (non-Anglo) name, where others had not. *Respect trumps harmony.*

Diversity vs inclusion

What's the difference? The way I like to think of it is that diversity is the ingredients in your recipe, all the different elements that come together. It's the mix. Inclusion is the finished product. It's the cake.

While getting the team mix right will achieve a much better outcome, it requires an understanding of *unconscious bias*—the attitudes, perspectives and stereotypes we accumulate through our life experience that can influence our decision making, particularly when we are under pressure. This pressure might be generated by an ambiguous situation, tiredness or a lack (or overload) of information. We need to think fast, so we fall back on our unconscious bias, which often leads to an inaccurate assessment based on flawed reasoning.

Unconscious bias can often mean only a narrow pool of candidates are interviewed for a job or promoted into senior roles. It limits diversity and inclusion in the workplace, which in turn blocks innovation.

Because we can't process all the information we receive at once, unconscious bias works as a reflex, inclining us towards quick judgements and rash assessments.

The first step in managing these hidden influencers is to recognise the common types of bias.

1. AFFINITY BIAS

Affinity bias leads us to favour people we feel we have a connection to or compatibility with. For example, we've worked for the same company or attended the same university, or we like the same kind of music. The other person reminds us of ourselves or someone we know and like.

Interactions with people we feel we share an affinity with will differ from those with people we feel less connected to. For example, in group assignments at school or university, we will be far more forgiving towards someone who isn't pulling their weight if we have an affinity with them, if we have something in common, than if we don't.

Similarly, in most volunteer organisations there is an expectation that everyone will attend weekly training to service equipment or practise team skills. It's part of the commitment. But sometimes we simply can't get there. If a person regularly misses training, and you have an affinity with them, you will be more likely to make excuses for this behaviour. If it's someone you have nothing in common with, however, it's easier to put down their non-attendance to a lack of commitment or laziness.

2. THE HALO EFFECT

The halo effect comes into play when we perceive one great thing about a person and let that golden glow colour our opinions of everything else we know about that person.

For example, if someone has received a prestigious award in their industry we tend to let this achievement influence how we view them more generally. They won a top industry award so they must be good.

3. THE HORNS EFFECT

Conversely, when our perception of someone is unduly influenced by what we perceive as a negative trait, the horns effect has taken over.

For example, if we don't approve of the way someone wears jeans and t-shirts to work we might assume they are generally slack and unprofessional, even though professionalism and competence are quite unrelated to the clothes we wear.

4. ATTRIBUTION BIAS

Attribution bias affects how we evaluate other people and their achievements. It can be particularly influential during recruitment.

When assessing ourselves, we tend to attribute our achievements to our hard work and personal qualities, while our failures are put down to external factors, including the obstructionism of other people.

When it comes to assessing other people, though, we often draw the opposite conclusion. We are more likely to consider the achievements of others a result of chance or unfair advantage, and their failings a result of their lack of commitment or personal qualities.

5. CONFIRMATION BIAS

Confirmation bias is the tendency to search for, interpret, focus on and remember information that aligns with our preconceived opinions. It confirms what we already think.

We subconsciously look for evidence to back up our own opinions, to show we are right about a person.

In Antarctica, the only recruitment decision I had to make was to choose a deputy station leader from among my wintering group. My natural inclination was to choose someone I had a lot in common with and felt I could work well with (affinity bias). We enjoyed the same music, we were the same age so we had similar childhood memories, and we laughed together a lot during training.

This wouldn't have been the best decision for the team, though. Why? Because we were so similar that he wouldn't have provided a real alternative perspective to mine. I felt that if people were uncomfortable discussing something with me, they needed to be able to turn to someone quite different from me. Since I was a young, tertiary-educated female, it just made sense to choose an older, on-the-tools male.

I had nothing much in common with my deputy leader, but this was possibly the best decision I made all year. He approached difficulties in a different way from me and when it was time for us to write up the performance reviews for our expedition team he often gave examples of great teamwork, and not so great behaviour, that I hadn't considered. So the end result was much broader and more well-rounded.

In a nutshell

- While demographic diversity is often more visible and apparent, it's cognitive diversity that can be the most challenging – and also the most rewarding. Diverse teams will always achieve a better outcome because they consider options and alternatives from a greater variety of viewpoints, a broader knowledge base and wider experience to arrive at a solution.
- When you are aware of unconscious bias, it is easier to counteract it.

The challenge of forming a team

When I first arrived in Hobart to begin my Antarctic service, I was told by a past expeditioner that we 'are brothers in arms and we are prepared to die for each other'. My response was, 'No, we are a federal government workplace and we don't break a nail for each other'.

This conception of 'inclusive leadership' is very common. Many leaders will focus on building their team by emphasising what they have in common. It's natural for a team leader to focus on getting the individuals to know and like each other. We all want to fit in, to share jokes, to work harmoniously shoulder-to-shoulder with others.

We often hear how we are more alike than we are different. Thinking about our similarities is great, but I want to shine a light on the differences your people will never agree on. As a leader, what do you do then? What if there is no common ground?

As one example, in recent years marriage equality has been a big issue and a source of much contention in Australia. Our Antarctic team included gay people as well as individuals who (mostly for religious reasons) opposed gay marriage. These people would never reach agreement on the subject of marriage equality. Nor did I expect them to.

We didn't need to reach consensus. We just needed to acknowledge and respect our differences.

Go beyond tolerance; respect that I'm different from you.

RECOGNISE EXTREME DIVERSITY, BOTH COGNITIVE AND DEMOGRAPHIC

Great diversity means natural connections between people may take time. If the only thing they have in common is the same employer, it may take a while to build affinity, if it happens at all. And that's okay. The most important thing is to treat one another respectfully.

When you start to think of diversity in both a cognitive and a demographic frame you soon realise every team is diverse, regardless of what they look like on the outside.

I work with a lot of engineering companies, and when I walk into the room it would be easy to typecast the group as a homogeneous one, comprising mostly Anglo-Saxon men aged in their forties and fifties. This may be true as far as it goes, but I could select three of the group randomly and find at least ten areas of difference between them.

THE PROBLEM WITH LOW DIVERSITY

In low-diversity environments you would expect high levels of harmony, and this may be the case, but when you scratch the surface you soon realise that teams are more diverse than you first might think, and often there are issues brewing beneath the surface.

I started my career in public relations. Back then it was an industry in which young women predominated. We really had a great time together and socialised outside work quite often; we celebrated birthdays with gusto, and we generally had a blast. In fact, there was never any conflict. But that was because the issues were ignored or glossed over to keep the peace and to maintain the fiction that we all loved each other.

This is not harmony. It's exactly why talented people walk out the door, to everyone's great surprise. People get tired of playing this game. It's the old mantra: 'If you have nothing nice to say, then don't say anything at all.' That may have worked well in the past, but it simply won't work in a modern, diverse team.

People need to know they can raise an issue and have it discussed in a mature, professional and realistic manner. Ignoring issues or telling people to 'suck it up' creates enormous problems, as we will discuss in the next section.

SUPER TUESDAY

In Antarctica we established Super Tuesday, a regular hourly spot on a Tuesday night when anyone could get up in front of the community and talk about a topic they were passionate or knowledgeable about. Topics ranged from paganism, living in Prague, and digital photography to learning Italian, the history of the Formula 1 Grand Prix, astronomy ... anything.

I had placed a sign-up sheet on the noticeboard in the foyer asking for people to volunteer to host a session, and I optimistically hoped we'd fill a few dates. Within two days the list was fully subscribed and we had 15 weeks of activities locked in.

These events were a huge success, but not for the reason I had initially intended. My original plan was simply to break up the monotony of the Antarctic winter by giving everyone something to look forward to each week. What happened was very different, and way more important.

As people showcased and shared their knowledge we learned much more about them, their experience, interests and abilities, over and above what we saw at work. It built respect in the team. It may not have changed how we felt about them as individuals, and perhaps they still weren't our 'cup of tea', but we could at least acknowledge and respect them for the diverse skills and talents we hadn't known about.

Case study: Carlton & United Breweries (CUB)

CUB has an excellent focus on people and culture, and often talks about the 'recipe for a successful team'. They identify six special ingredients for their teamwork, but my favourite is this one:

> 'Diversity in every way. The more opinions and perspectives that are shared, the greater the range of ideas we have to work with and the better the outcomes for all. Everyone at CUB has a voice and we want to hear each and every one of them.'

In a nutshell

- To be an inclusive leader, actively seek out different views and be aware of your own biases.
- Some people will push your buttons, no matter what. You cannot control their behaviour, but you can control your reaction to it. Manage your personal boundaries, recognise when you are feeling irritated or exasperated, and remove yourself from the situation temporarily and diplomatically.
- People have a host of skills, knowledge and abilities that we may never hear about in a work or volunteer context. If you're able to unearth these skills, even through simple conversation, it will build understanding and respect in the team.

PART I
Respect trumps harmony

CHAPTER 1
Harmony — the road to mediocre

What is harmony?

One dictionary definition describes harmony as the 'consistent, orderly or pleasing arrangement of parts'. In social terms, what we commonly understand by harmony is a state in which people get along together, are nice to each other and coexist peacefully without arguing or fighting.

To use a musical metaphor, harmony is created when different voices singing different notes combine to pleasing effect. Disparate elements come together in a planned way. It's also the product of our efforts to understand one another, work together and cater for our differences. A choirmaster knows the tenor can't hit that high A note and a contralto can pitch in.

All sports team members have specialist skills, and the skilled coach harnesses their individual strengths, acknowledging and capitalising on their differences.

Differences, such as sexual orientation, can play a big part in people's self-identity. For lots of people their career or work has a significant role in their self-identity (it's why you'll never hear someone say, 'Oh, I never knew you were a Qantas pilot'. If you meet a Qantas pilot you'll know about it soon enough, because they'll tell you!). Just kidding.

For others, it's their ancestry, ethnicity or culture that they believe largely defines them. For many white Australians, their culture—historical or current—has no real impact on their lives, while for Indigenous Australians their aboriginality is understandably often a huge part of their identity.

We need to be able to respect and not discount these critical differences.

This is how respect trumps harmony. Respect is an INPUT; harmony is an OUTPUT.

Pulling in the same direction

So if harmony isn't the magic ingredient in team performance, what is? The answer isn't straightforward. According to Mark de Rond at Cambridge University, two features of teams appear to contribute significantly to higher-than-usual performance. These are psychological safety: 'teams that provide safe spaces for frank and constructive conversation are far less likely to see people hide mistakes or illnesses, or self-censor for fear of looking incompetent'. He found too that effective teams 'know precisely what matters, and who it matters to, leveraging this to socialise newcomers, to make tough calls, and to measure progress'.

Case study: Cambridge University boat crew

The Cambridge University boat crew has only one constitutional reason for existence: to beat rivals Oxford in the annual boat race on the Thames, which has been run since 1829.

This single-minded focus means they apply just one criterion when making decisions: will doing this help us win the race, yes or no? A variant on this question, colloquially referred to among the rowing fraternity as the Stephens Test, is 'will it make the boat go faster?' If the answer is affirmative, we do it. If not, we don't.

Organisations today are generally vastly more complex and con-voluted than a rowing team, particularly matrix organisations with multiple reporting lines. Yet might it not be useful to try, as a team, to articulate an equivalent 'test' to provide focus, to help build a sense of identity and to help team members make choices?

British Cycling's Team Sky boss Dave Brailsford says, 'I don't spend a nanosecond worrying whether they [the cyclists] get on. People talk about having team unity and team harmony.' But the sport, he suggests, is not a harmonious domain. 'This is a gritty environment where people are pushing really hard. What you need is goal harmony, and there's a big difference between the two.'

We often assume that the best teams are those that get along best, but of course that's not always the case, and nor should it be. The challenge for the creative leader is to manage the tensions (and sometimes even introduce them) to get the best results.

'Do not criticise,' we are told, is one of the most important tenets of brainstorming. This simply underscores the fact that criticism and creative abrasion can have significant effects on the quality of ideas generated. Harmony overrides results.

In a nutshell

There is an assumption in many teams that we all have to get along all the time. We do not. We don't have to love each other; we don't even have to like each other. We just need to treat each other with respect. Courtesy and respect.

Why a focus on harmony can be dangerous

What does a lack of respect look like?

Respect, like offence, is personal. What I might find incredibly disrespectful might not concern the next person at all. What each of us finds disrespectful or offensive will differ according to our values and life experiences.

Very often the person we believe has demonstrated a lack of respect is totally oblivious to it. When we shine a light on their behaviour it can be the first time they've reflected on it. Whether they modify their behaviour as a result is completely in their hands, but at least we have drawn attention to the impact it has on us.

Let's look briefly at three different environments in which this can take place.

1. SCHOOLS

I recently asked a school principal if he could think of examples of behaviour that were seen as disrespectful by some members of staff but totally acceptable by others. The first example he thought of was yard duty. This requires that one teacher take the first half-hour shift, from 1.30 pm to 2.00 pm, when the next person on the roster takes over. But it didn't always happen like that. Some second-shift staff were coming onto the yard at 2.05 or 2.10, because at the start of their shift they were busy filling their drink bottle, collecting their high-vis vest and putting on their sunscreen, which meant they regularly appeared in the school yard a few minutes late. This was a source of increasing frustration for the first-shift staff because it significantly cut into their lunch break. In some cases, by the time they got back to the staff room they had only 20 minutes before their next class.

We talked about whether this was an issue about 'only a few minutes', or something more significant—specifically, a lack of respect. The issue was raised at the next staff meeting and after much discussion it was agreed that if you are required on yard duty at two o'clock, then that is when you should be actually in the yard patrolling.

The most important part of this scenario was to raise the issue and discuss it in a professional and open manner, rather than to keep ignoring it, allowing the discontent to fester. *Respect trumps harmony.*

2. HOSPITALS

A hospital is a very challenging workplace. The stakes are high and patients' emotions are frequently running wild. It can be an incredibly stressful environment, but it is still a workplace, where every staff member should be treated with respect, irrespective of their role.

I recently worked with a private hospital team that was having a significant issue with a specialist surgeon. His manner was brash and abrasive, especially towards the nursing staff, and he was regularly late for his surgeries, which had a knock-on effect for other medical staff who had booked the theatre.

When I asked why no one had raised the issue, I was told it was because he was highly skilled and in demand, and therefore generated significant revenue for the hospital. In other words, we turn a blind eye to keep the peace.

As we discussed possible solutions I learned that the surgeon in question was always the first cab off the rank in theatre. He had the opening slot booked every time he was operating. The trouble was, he was also consulting with patients in his rooms and these appointments often went over time, as they do. His late arrival at theatre pushed his surgery back and consequently a block of surgeries booked after him were then pushed back in a domino effect. When I asked if there was a particular reason he was booked in first I was told there wasn't—it was just his personal preference.

Whether or not the specialist was aware of the impact his behaviour was having remained unexplored. But after much discussion his slot was moved to later in the day. Ironically, he was fine with this as he found it relieved him of the pressure to wrap up his consulting appointments and get to the theatre.

3. FAMILIES

Anyone with children will know the daily grind of getting kids to clean up after themselves. With smaller children it's understandable, but as they get older and become perfectly capable of picking up after themselves it becomes an ongoing battle—for most parents anyway. When they come home from school, drop their bag on the floor, throw jackets on the bed, grab food out of the cupboard and leave the wrappers lying around it is usually easier to grit your teeth and just deal with it yourself. I know I tended to do this. It was the path of least resistance. But then it struck me that one of our roles as parents is to teach our children what respect looks like, so by keeping the peace and harmony and cleaning up after them ourselves, we are actually doing them a disservice. Our role is to teach them respect, and that often comes, however briefly, at the price of harmony.

What happens when disrespectful behaviour is not addressed?

If the behaviour is allowed to continue, it becomes normalised and part of the culture. For example, if one or two people regularly arrive late for meetings, you can be fairly sure that in a short time others will join them. Why wouldn't they? Why should they be left waiting in the meeting room for the regular late arrivals? So the behaviour becomes embedded and soon every 10.00 am meeting will start at 10.15 to allow for the latecomers.

Issues left unattended will often escalate. I recently encountered an 'all staff' email sent to a corporate head office team of more than 200 people. It was sent, evidently not for the first time, to raise a recurrent issue: 'Whoever is leaving their gym clothes in the disabled toilets after you've had a shower following your ride to work', it read, 'could you please stop!'

In all my years of working with teams, I have never once had a person tell me they don't receive enough emails. Never. They might complain about not being kept informed about significant projects, but no one has ever suggested they would like to increase the volume of emails they receive. Certainly no one has ever expressed a desire for emails that are totally irrelevant to them. So I can well imagine people's exasperation on receiving this email about the gym clothes when they have never, ever, ridden a bike to work or used the disabled toilets.

I'm no detective but I'm confident that most of us, with a few minutes and a few pertinent questions, could narrow down the field to a pretty short list of potential culprits in this case. *They* are the people you speak to. Don't turn a small triangle into an email pyramid scheme.

What happens when harmony is the dominant driver?

When the overwhelming focus is on harmony and keeping the peace, teams will adapt to accommodate the behaviour. They soon learn not to create friction and will turn a blind eye and ignore poor behaviour, which can then escalate ... until eventually a royal commission into misconduct is launched!

Often teams fail to address a lack of respect because it's hard and confronting, and it takes time and energy. Most people avoid one-on-one confrontation by taking what they see as the path of least resistance, which means tolerating disrespectful behaviour rather than challenging it.

This issue is particularly difficult in volunteer organisations. Many of these groups are located in regional and rural areas where there isn't an overabundance of people putting their hands up to volunteer. Yet, for example, to ensure the safety of the local community and visitors to the area we need a fully staffed SES team, fire and rescue service, and St John Ambulance. Teams must be in place to respond to emergencies and in a small population everyone needs to share this load—and sometimes this includes people who don't have the aptitude or disposition for emergency response roles.

An easy option is to move the volunteer displaying negative behaviour into a non-operational role away from the rest of the team, but this is tricky when the person signed up to volunteer because they wanted to be on the front line of the response, not working in the back office. So rather than ignoring this individual's poor behaviour, it *must* be addressed for the benefit of the entire team. You may lose one volunteer. But that's a whole lot better than the whole team walking out.

Set the scene: leaders need to clearly communicate that *respect trumps harmony* and articulate just what distinguishes respectful and disrespectful behaviour for the team. Each team will differ, so coming to a consensus on expectations and non-negotiables ensures clarity for everyone.

A cultural collision

One summer afternoon in Antarctica, I was standing in the foyer pinning up a roster on the noticeboard when I heard an almighty commotion. Turning around I saw Jess, a young (and evidently very angry) scientist, storming past. She was carrying a large plastic bucket stuffed with scientific equipment and wearing a backpack.

A few seconds later, Bob, who at 65 years old was one of the more senior members of the team, walked past. He looked chastened, but also visibly upset.

What was that all about?

Then the penny dropped. I'd heard Jess mutter, 'My arms aren't bloody painted on!' and it didn't take me long to work out what had just happened. Bob had opened the door for Jess to help her out. Now, Jess is a very competent and capable woman. She lives for weeks on the Antarctic plateau taking scientific measurements. She's tough and can look after herself, and if she ever needs help she'll ask for it. I concluded, rightly as it turned out, that she had taken offence when Bob opened the door for her. She saw it as patronising and demeaning and reacted accordingly.

As I was standing there taking this in I realised I had three options: I could pretend I hadn't noticed and just ignore it (I'd certainly done that before). I could wait till Jess was out of earshot and try to defuse the situation with Bob by using humour and saying something like 'Pfft, kids these days, hey?' Or I could step in and manage the situation.

I chose option three. It was a relatively minor incident that I decided was not about gender or youth—or chauvinism. Bob didn't open the door because Jess was young and female. He opened the door because he saw she was carrying a heavy load. It was about respect and I would expect every single one of the expedition team to do the same.

While I understood Jess's irritation, and how her past experience of being a female scientist in a male-dominated field might have informed her response, I needed to convey to her that in this particular instance her reaction was inappropriate. She didn't need to react with anger. A simple 'I've got this' would have sufficed.

I got involved in the situation because I needed to clarify my expectation as leader, that I expected that every single person would be considerate enough to open a door for someone carrying a load of equipment. It was about both respect and safety. I escalated the incident because *respect trumps harmony*.

In a nutshell

- In all the best teams there's an element of constructive tension. A team that prioritises harmony won't hold people accountable or confront poor behaviour. Results are secondary and performance is mediocre at best. The only way to build a high-performance culture is to hold people accountable for their results, behaviour and responsibilities.

- In a team that focuses solely on harmony, any improvement is a result of sheer luck, not culture. Improvement often comes out of failure, yet if the culture is to sweep mistakes under the carpet because the leader is either unwilling or unable to address the problem, then there is no opportunity to identify, assess and learn from the failure.

CHAPTER 2
Change is now business as usual

Adapt or perish. It's not the strongest who survive, but those who are most responsive to change.

Working with Millennials

The Millennial generation is now the largest cohort in the workplace. They are tech savvy, ambitious and often restless, so what's the secret to retaining them?

Like previous generations, Millennials (also known as Gen Y) want to feel valued at work, enjoy time with family and friends, and engage in a variety of hobbies and sports. But they have specific qualities that set them apart from other generations. Formative experiences have shaped this cohort into a very different workforce, and employers must recognise and respond to this change or risk losing talented staff again and again. But how? Here are some useful approaches:

1. **Understand what drives them.** The Millennial generation came of age during the global financial crisis and experienced first-hand the impact of redundancies

and retrenchment on their families. They watched on as cost-cutting took precedence over loyalty. So it's no surprise that they now place personal needs above corporate interests. They need meaning and purpose at work and require line-of-sight to the business goals. They want to understand explicitly how they contribute to the greater team effort, so show them.

2. **Provide constant communication opportunities.** These digital natives are always 'on'. They are technologically connected in ways previous generations never were, and they want, and expect, to listen and be heard—whenever, wherever. Anonymous, micro-feedback platforms provide immediate real-time opportunities for staff to innovate, provide feedback, contribute or complain. These platforms are also a lot easier to utilise, and far less expensive and cumbersome than staff engagement surveys.

3. **Stretch them, challenge them and harness their inner Zuckerberg.** The Millennials have grown up watching entrepreneurs hit lofty heights and amass immense wealth and status—all before they turn 30. The barriers to entrepreneurial success have never been lower and the 'why not?' attitude has never been stronger. Acknowledge this and shower your Millennials with professional development opportunities, particularly in-house mentoring. This cohort is incredibly diverse and enjoys teamwork, so create temporary project teams to innovate and solve difficult problems. Many tech companies set aside a day each month for digital solutions forums where staff are encouraged to be creative and think audaciously to create the next big thing.

4. **Ditch the annual reviews.** Millennials have grown up with broadband, smartphones, laptops and social media as the norm. They want instant access to ideas and information but also instant feedback on their own performance. For older generations it may seem like they have a constant need for attention and reassurance, but it's more complex than that. They have grown up giving

14

opinions and offering thoughts and they appreciate receiving the same in return. They are also quite happy to receive the feedback electronically: 41 per cent prefer electronic to face-to-face communication, according to a recent PWC report, 'Millennials in the workplace'.

5. **Teach them to lead.** For the first time in history we will have younger generations managing older generations. This is fertile ground for intergenerational conflict. To avoid potential issues, every person moving into a management role should be given leadership development training. More than ever, leaders will need the skills to be able to resolve interpersonal conflict and negotiate outcomes. Equip your Millennials for success by giving them the fundamental leadership tools of resilience, self-awareness and decision-making skills. This isn't an add-on, it's foundational. If you want them to stick around, they need to feel competent and confident in their own ability to handle difficult situations.

6. **Ramp up collaboration.** For Millennials, their instant access to knowledge and information has taught them that no one is indispensable, no one is the font of all knowledge and there is much power in collaboration. In fact, more than 75 per cent of Millennials report that they prefer working collaboratively. They are more technologically connected than anyone before them, yet they prefer a physical workspace where they can see and be seen. Provide opportunities for varied project work, including corporate-wide initiatives, and watch your Millennials shine.

Like the Emperor penguins, businesses too need to adapt to the prevailing environment to ensure their survival. This is especially the case in retaining Millennial staff, who in 2020 will represent more than half the global workforce. To survive, today's organisations require not just the hands of their workers but their hearts and minds too.

Managing former peers and friends

One of the toughest leadership challenges, especially for emerging leaders or people in regional communities where you live and work together, is how to manage former peers and friends.

It's a very common challenge, and it's hard—really hard.

It's especially difficult in Australia where we have a strong culture of mateship and 'getting along'. But remember: *respect trumps harmony*. It's always better to address an issue head on, no matter how tricky, than to let it slide and fester, allowing resentment to build. So, in the interest of building respect in teams, here is my advice on how to handle the challenge of managing your mates.

IT'S NOT YOU, IT'S ME ...

It's finally happened. You've worked hard, delivered your work on time and on budget. You've come up with a great initiative or two and now it's all paid off—you've been rewarded with a promotion.

The good news is you've been recognised for your dedication and ability and you are now a leader. The bad news is you've been recognised for your dedication and ability and you are now a leader. Yep, it's a double-edged sword. The reaction of your peers will vary too: some of your cohort will be happy for you; others will be ambivalent; still others may feel resentment, particularly if they had applied for the same job but missed out.

Things have changed dramatically, and the most important thing is to recognise this. They will never be the same again. As a friend and peer, you may have been privy to personal information your manager wasn't. You may know, for example, that the late afternoon 'meeting' your colleague attends every second Friday isn't a meeting at all but rather an early pass home. Well, now it's your problem to manage.

Moving into a leadership role is a transition. It takes time, and a whole lot of effort, to straddle the dual role of team leader and colleague.

Here's what you need to do:

1. **Address the elephant in the room: things have changed.** The power dynamic has shifted and as their leader you now have input into important decisions that have a significant impact on the careers and wellbeing of your people, such as training opportunities, L & D, rewards and incentives, even annual leave. Be sensitive to the new power you yield.

2. **Pull back from social activities and events outside work.** I have always had a policy of only attending social functions that my entire team is invited to, such as Christmas lunch and end-of-year dinners. This is to avoid any perception of favouritism. It's unwise to share movies and dinners and winery tours with one of your staff while having no involvement outside work with others, because it creates a sense of 'us and them'. If you have been lifelong friends with a colleague, you need to set some ground rules for your friendship outside of work, such as not discussing work or colleagues, being discreet and not posting photos on social media. Remember, your leadership responsibility isn't over just because you're 'off the clock'. Stay cool.

3. **No triangles.** Never discuss other colleagues (peers, other departments, senior managers or executives) with your staff. Office gossip among peers is damaging enough, but I've seen more than one career implode when a new leader decided it was okay to whinge to their own staff about the exec team. As a leader, what you say has extra volume; it will be taken as 'given' and will be repeated. Be warned.

4. **Build a new network of your own peers.** Leadership is often lonely, and you need opportunities to discuss tactics, seek counsel, even vent about frustrating stakeholders. Set up a time to have a coffee with one of your peers and build that relationship. It will keep you sane.

5. **Volunteer to chair a company-wide initiative, team or project.** Most organisations have projects dedicated to health, safety and environmental outcomes, for example. By taking on a leadership role you will build your credibility throughout the business and be seen to be ... a leader.

6. **If possible, ask your current manager to announce your new position.** This establishes your authority publicly and confirms you have the support of management.

7. **Set the tone early by arranging a team meeting to look at the short- and long-term goals for the team.** Seek input from your people and remind them a new leader is always an opportunity for positive change. It's a great time to discuss your and their concerns and resolve any issues. Also meet with your team one-on-one to discuss their ambitions and challenges. Then schedule regular one-on-one catch-ups (two hours a month is great). This reassures your team that your initial attention wasn't just a one-off.

A NOTE ON THE STAFF MEMBER WHO APPLIED FOR YOUR JOB AND MISSED OUT

If you find someone is testing your authority by, say, coming in late or spending too much time on social media, step in immediately—but with a light touch. Address the issue straight away, but do it with respect and sensitivity. You don't need to assert your authority; you already have it. If the behaviour persists then you need to call it out, but address very specific examples. Use your LADAR (language radar; see chapter 8) and avoid absolutes like 'always' or 'everyone'. Use facts and take out the emotion.

Case study: Vanguard

Vanguard is a global investment company built on a low-cost model and is client owned, so all profits are directed to clients rather than outside owners.

Vanguard very proudly, and very specifically, seek diversity in their 'crew'. They believe it's a competitive advantage. One of their values is: 'We welcome debate'. They actively seek out constructive disagreement, and when things go wrong they 'don't ask who [but] ask why?' (DAWAW) to search for the root cause.

At the senior levels the team is keen to generate debate in strategy discussions, which is why they created 'Devil's Advocacy' sessions in which a senior executive identifies a business issue and selects a team of staff to debate from opposite sides of the issue. It's a simple and powerful tool for overcoming conformity in thinking and is very useful in teams where consensus is valued above robust debate. It also ensures that varied and often conflicting perspectives are factored into decision making. It's very effective – try it.

Families, sports and community groups — we're all in it together

Every one of us is part of a team, commonly in our paid job, but we are at the same time part of a family and a community. Many also give their time in a voluntary capacity to groups such as St John Ambulance, SES, rural fire services, surf lifesaving clubs and any number of other charitable and community initiatives. More than a few of us play a team sport too.

Whether it's in paid or unpaid work, sports or community groups, team activities play a significant role in our lives. And here the same principles apply; in fact, they may be even more important in these group settings given the often greater diversity of the participants.

As I mentioned earlier, a culture in which *respect trumps harmony* is vital in volunteer organisations, but maintaining it can be tricky. Many of these groups are located in regional and rural areas. Teams must be in place to respond to emergencies. With a small population it falls to everyone to share this load—and sometimes this includes people who lack the aptitude or disposition for such a role. Where this results in poor behaviour, rather than ignoring it, for the benefit of the whole team it's much better to address it.

The incredible diversity found in many volunteer teams also means you need to consider communicating in different ways, such as through team meetings, one-on-one coaching, visual aids and newsletters. People receive and process information differently. Think, for example, about the best ways to reach those for whom English is their second language.

Case study: Volunteer fire brigades

Tanya works with several volunteer fire brigades, where her role focuses on leadership. She deals with the people side of firefighting, and often works with the more vulnerable brigades that have difficulties recruiting and retaining members.

She introduced 'no triangles' in a number of groups experiencing high levels of conflict. 'Often', she told me, 'there is a disconnect between members and the leadership teams. My job is to try to resolve that problem, and I thought encouraging direct conversations, with *no triangles*, would help.'

Tanya introduced the *no triangles* model in areas where there was lots of whingeing rather than addressing the issue directly with the person concerned. Recognising that the brigade members had very different backgrounds, education levels and socioeconomic circumstances, she decided to use visual aids as well. The idea was to encourage members either to address the problem themselves or to take it to a leader—not simply to complain to another member. They put up the no triangles poster on the wall in the brigades as a reminder.

They also held a short workshop to discuss their values. What does respect mean? What does it look like?

Results

'One brigade in a very low socioeconomic area is quite isolated. We had to take really small steps, but *no triangles* has had a really big impact and the culture has picked up really well.'

Repetition of the message was very important, as was ensuring it got out to all members. 'Each brigade has on average about 30 members, and we needed to make sure all of them heard the same message. We developed our own posters. One gap we recognised was that the team leaders and managers needed more guidance around how to have the conversations. So that's our next priority.'

PART II
The three pillars to build respect in teams

CHAPTER 3
No triangles: the importance of direct conversations

Integrity is critical to the success of a team, and a lack of it leads to poor performance. Teams and organisations need simple ways to encourage the right behaviours, and the tools to call out behaviours that are counterproductive. One simple teamwork tool can increase staff productivity by up to 40 per cent.

I have been researching the link between integrity and productivity for 13 years, and the business case is clear: more than 90 per cent of people surveyed agreed that a culture of *no triangles* would have a significant impact on their work productivity.

No triangles is the practice of conducting direct conversations when issues or problems arise. *I don't speak to you about him, and you don't speak to me about her. If I have an issue with someone I go directly to that person, I don't take it to a third party.* Implementing a *no triangles* culture builds integrity in a team and ensures we treat each other with respect.

In its simplest form it means if someone has upset you at work, or in your family or community group, you have the courtesy and integrity to take your concern directly to that person, rather than complaining to a third party.

Think about how it feels when you have unknowingly upset someone, especially at work, but only discover it, quite out of context, from a third party. It's horrible.

No triangles is about demonstrating the courage, courtesy and professionalism to go straight to the source and have a direct, honest and respectful conversation with the person concerned.

When we create, or participate in, a triangle it indicates a number of things. Firstly, it suggests that the complainer lacks the courage or confidence to conduct a direct conversation about something that's bothering them. It reflects poorly on them because it is disrespectful.

Secondly, if your role in the triangle is that of willing listener, you are implicitly endorsing this behaviour. It sends the message to the complainer that going behind someone's back to get something done is an acceptable way of dealing with issues. It can also be interpreted that you tacitly agree with their complaint.

Lastly, when an often inaccurate, emotionally charged version of this ill-advised exchange reaches the target of the complaint via the third party, their relationship with the complainer is damaged, sometimes permanently.

Triangle conversations erode trust and confidence, create misinformation, breed innuendo and perpetuate a culture of disrespect. They also promote the idea that back-room conversations (rather than direct, professional communications) are an acceptable means of getting things done.

Four types of triangles

There are four types, or sources, of triangles that I see most often in the workplace:

1. **Malicious gossip.** Through spreading half-truths and falsehoods, a malicious gossip deliberately sets out to undermine someone and damage their reputation. This is

probably the most insidious form of triangle and it points to deep issues in the culture. If you've got this happening in your workplace, then you should probably stop reading here and go straight to the implementation section! Gossip that is deliberately designed to drag down another person or team is toxic, whether it's in the workplace, at home or in your social circles.

2. **Idle gossip.** This behaviour is generally less destructive in the short term, but it's still something you want to deal with promptly. Speculation, innuendo, passing on bits of private information (or misinformation) can be really harmful to relationships when it finds its way back to the target (and it usually does!). It erodes trust and confidence, which is the last thing you want in your team.

3. **Complaining.** One of your team members comes to you to complain about a colleague. They don't want you to do anything about it … no, they just think you should know. In other words, they're just whingeing. In Antarctica I realised early on that this type of complaint, or dobbing as children call it, would affect my own health. It's exhausting, but worse still, if you won't speak to the person, and you don't want me to do so either, then nothing changes! How can it?

4. **Answer shopping.** Now, I'm not implying this happens in your team, but it has happened in almost every team I've worked in! Someone approaches you with a request. You don't give them the answer they want, so they go around you or over your head. They shop around until they get the answer they want. Bad. We know why people do it: because it works. But you'll never forget how it feels to be 'the person who said no'. It's so disempowering, and it erodes trust in a team. Unfortunately, today's multiple reporting lines and matrix organisations mean decision-making authority is not always so black and white. But the rule of thumb is 'line-management is king'.

The most important part of implementing *no triangles* is that every person in the team commits to it; every single person must put their hand up and say yes, we understand and are committed to practising *no triangles*. Then the next time someone tries to engage you in one of those 'she said' or 'he did' conversations, *bam*... you have a tool to manage it. You can say, 'But I saw you put up your hand and commit to *no triangles*, so why are you talking to me about this? Why aren't you talking to her [him] about it?'

Answer shopping, too, needs to stop. You may need to say, 'I'm not accountable for that decision, you need to go and speak to [so and so]'. Send them straight back to the correct person. *No triangles.*

It's *always* better to deal with issues directly. It's about culture, but it's also about productivity. You don't want people hanging around and complaining about someone's behaviour with no plan to do anything about it. That creates an even bigger distraction! So, if you want to lead a productive team, defined by a culture of respect, you need to practise *no triangles*.

In my experience, senior leadership teams often have more triangles at the executive table and in the board room than anywhere else. This can almost always be explained by competition for resources. With finite budgets there's a need to build a strong business case for funding, whether it's for more staff, projects or anything else. One path to achieving this is to diminish the appeal of another executive's project.

Case study: Senior leaders at war

A financial services company was developing a new product they hoped would become a game-changer in the insurance industry. So far it was unproven, but early focus group sessions and robust analysis showed it had huge potential.

The leader of the project was asked to present the latest findings at a meeting of the executive team. She was slightly anxious but knew the product was strong, and she had prepared thoroughly.

Imagine her reaction when the chief marketing officer tore the project apart – very publicly. She had arrived at the meeting expecting a collaborative process, but suddenly it had become highly adversarial. She was stunned.

In our debrief we established that the key issue was differing interests and competition for resources. The CMO had a full slate of projects, so this new one, no matter how great it was or how much revenue it would drive, was problematic for him. It would mean diverting staff and funding away from the existing and agreed marketing plan.

To move from an adversarial position to a collaborative one, a few things need to happen:

1. Both parties need to understand the competing interests. They need to be aware of the key performance indicators the other person is held accountable for and recognise that this is their priority and that's why they are acting the way they are.

2. Both parties need to understand resource constraints. Almost always, a new project will require that funding be diverted away from an existing project. A strategic decision must be made around what work should be stopped to make way for the new project.

3. A statement of agreed facts should be developed that accounts for:

   • the strategic priorities for the business

   • resource availability

   • the full bill of work — the total picture.

Once you have agreed on these facts it becomes much easier to negotiate on the variables. That is, if a project is a strategic priority for the business, then it takes precedence. New, less strategic projects can be considered, but only if the resources are available and won't be diverted from an agreed priority. If you're unsure which project is of greater strategic importance, take it to the executive team to decide. That's their job.

CHAPTER 4
The bacon war: what seems trivial could be titanic

Many of you will have heard me talk about 'the bacon war' from my time in Antarctica. At the time I didn't even know it was happening until one of the diesel mechanics came to see me and suggested I call a station meeting on how to cook the bacon on Mondays, when the chef has the morning off. Bewildered, I asked, 'Why?' 'Because the plumbers like it crispy and the diesel mechanics like it soft', he explained, 'and the plumbers are cooking it crispy and the diesos are cooking it soft, and we need to have a meeting so you can decide how it should be cooked'.

A full meeting. To talk about bacon.

Asking around, though, I soon realised this wasn't really about the bacon at all. There was a deeper issue around respect. These two teams had already experienced some conflict over the use of vehicles, which was now manifesting itself in *the bacon war*, with each side convinced the other was cooking the bacon in such a way as to deliberately annoy them.

So it was actually about respect.

The way I figured this out was by using root cause analysis, or 'the 5 Whys'. Here's how it works:

1. Why does it matter that the plumbers cook the bacon crispy and you prefer it soft?
   Because they never do what we ask them to.

2. Why do you say that?
   Because we ask them not to throw their tools in the ute and they still do it.

3. Why does that matter?
   Because it creates more work for us in servicing the vehicle.

4. Why is that an issue?
   Because we already have a full workload and they are adding to it by not listening to us.

5. Why don't they listen to you?
   They never do, because they don't respect us.

Aha!

In workplaces, homes and wherever people gather and interact there are moments, both large and small, that determine how the group functions. But it's the little things that most often build or destroy a culture, because the little things are usually symptoms of deeper issues.

Every workplace has its own 'bacon wars': dirty coffee cups in the office sink drive people to despair; overnight traders in investments banks leave their pizza boxes lying around for the staff in the morning to pick up; or it's mobile phones left to ring out, or people using a pool vehicle and bringing it back with an empty tank, or people who habitually turn up late for meetings … the list is endless. On the surface these issues may seem insignificant, but dig a little deeper and you'll find they are often symptoms of a bigger cultural problem around teamwork and respect. The distraction will almost certainly affect both productivity and harmony.

'I don't get it', someone told me recently. 'By the time someone puts up a notice saying, "Your mother doesn't work here, put your dishes in the dishwasher", they could have just put them away themselves.' He didn't understand. It's not about the dishes, it's about respect. Respect for other people's time. And the perception that 'my time is more valuable than yours'.

Remember that 'all staff' email I mentioned earlier about the gym clothes left in the disabled toilets? I bet you can think of a trivial issue that was ignored and festered and became bigger than it should have simply because no one demonstrated leadership and stepped in to solve the problem. Do you have a staff member who escalates every issue to their manager without taking personal accountability? Or a manager who won't deal with someone's poor behaviour even though it is affecting the whole team? These are all examples of leadership gone wrong. Thankfully, there is a simple solution. It takes just five seconds to get it right, and it could change the way you lead.

The Step In, Step Back model

We cannot intervene in every single workplace issue, so knowing what to do and when to do it is a crucial skill for leaders everywhere to learn. Get it right and everything runs smoothly, but get it wrong and disaster may be just around the corner. Leadership is about knowing what to do in a specific situation. Do I intervene or step back? Do I escalate or defuse a situation? Here's where the Step In, Step Back model (see figure 1, overleaf) proves useful. When you're faced with a dilemma, uncertain how to proceed, take five seconds to ask yourself two questions:

1. How many people does it affect?
2. Does it impact on the team's values?

The answer to these two questions will determine your course of action: step back, defuse, step in or escalate.

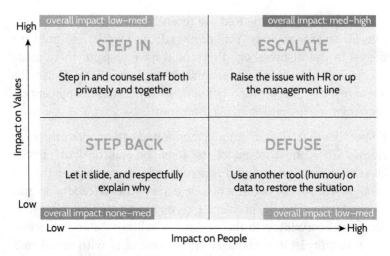

Figure 1: the Step In, Step Back model

STEP BACK

If the issue or situation impacts only one, two or a handful of people and has no impact on your values, then you can step back. Leaders simply don't have the time to become involved in every workplace issue or interpersonal conflict. Your time and energy needs to be channelled to where it will have the most impact, and that's not resolving every minor workplace or interpersonal dispute. In Antarctica, I was once asked by an expeditioner to call a team meeting to discuss the fact that one person was eating food with their fingers and not using cutlery. This issue affected only one person, and it surely had no impact on our core values, so I declined. But, importantly, I also explained why I would not get involved.

DEFUSE

If the issue or situation affects a large number of people, but again has no impact on your values, then you need to defuse it. Take the heat out of the situation by using relevant arguments and explaining the simple facts. Humour can sometimes be a useful tool in this scenario. The aim is to stop the distraction. The issue isn't important—as you have rightly decided—and it's taking up valuable time and energy.

STEP IN

If the situation impacts only one or two people *but* does involve a core team value, then you need to step in. I faced a situation that involved just two staff members, but the issue was about showing respect, the number one value in our team. So I got involved. I took each person aside separately and privately explained why it was such a big deal and clarified my expectations of their behaviour.

ESCALATE

If the behaviour impacts many people as well as your core values (respect, teamwork, accountability—whatever it is your team values most highly), then you need to escalate it, either to your line manager or to HR, or both. If the buck stops with you, then you need to meet it head on.

THE GREY AREAS IN BETWEEN

Of course, not every situation fits neatly into one of these four quadrants, and that's where judgement comes into play. But developing good judgement takes time and experience; most importantly, it requires reflection: What did I get right? What could I have done differently?

People look for consistency and predictability in their leaders. Apply this rule of thumb regularly and teach it to your people. The Step In, Step Back model is a great tool for helping leaders to get it right the first time.

How you like your bacon is, without doubt, a first-world issue and while it wouldn't affect the safety of the team, it could certainly affect our productivity and the delivery of our works program if left to fester. I asked for 10 minutes to think through what was going on here. As a leader you must take care of these little things, because often they surface as a symptom of a deeper issue. I had to manage the situation quickly in order to stop an escalating feud.

Take care of the little things and build respect along the way… because *respect trumps harmony*, every time.

In a nutshell

Here's a quick recap on how to manage your bacon wars:

- Don't let minor altercations build up. These things have a habit of bubbling away beneath the surface but when they explode watch out! Early intervention is the key.
- Deal only with the facts and leave out the emotion. Always base your analysis on things you can observe or deduce, rather than on anecdotes or complaints.
- Ask around and determine if and how it impacts your values and how many people it affects. Once you've decided to address the issue it won't take long to get feedback from people who are affected.
- Then use the Step In, Step Back model. If you're unsure which quadrant the problem lies in, start with conjecture until your views become firmer.

CHAPTER 5

Lead without a title: hold on to your talented staff and share the load

A question I'm often asked is, 'How can I show leadership when I'm not yet a leader?'

The answer is simple. Leadership isn't a title, it's a behaviour. You're a leader because of your thoughts and actions. You can show leadership regardless of your official role or title. In fact, the quickest and best way to become a leader is to start thinking and acting like one.

How do you do that? By showing big leadership in small moments. It's the moments that people remember, and it's the moments that inspire trust and confidence and commitment in the people around you. I call them *moments that matter*, and they are the subject of the next chapter.

Having 'leader' or 'manager' in your formal title doesn't automatically make you a leader, any more than not having such a title means you're not a leader. Leadership is a way of being, a way of behaving. It is seeing what needs to be done and doing it.

The aim of the contemporary leader is to develop more leaders, not more followers. It's about supporting and influencing the people around you, whether that's at home or at work or when volunteering in a community organisation. That's leadership, and you can demonstrate leadership in the smallest of moments.

In today's busy workplace, where everything is moving at the speed of light and we're all being asked to take on more tasks and projects and meet ever tighter deadlines, everyone needs to take a leadership role from time to time. To build respect in a team it's critical everyone feels heard, and equally, everyone feels a responsibility for the team's success.

You might think you're not paid to be a leader and you might prefer to work alone, but these thoughts limit your ability to operate at a higher level. To be respected you need to contribute, to be part of the team, to offer powerful solutions for yourself and the team, and you need to be able to influence the people around you.

Ask yourself, 'How do I lead myself to get better results?' This kind of higher-level question is a sign of a great leader. You've probably heard someone say, 'You make the decision, that's why you're paid big bucks'?

Well, actually no, it's not. The reason you're paid the big bucks isn't for the strategy and the innovation and the decision making, though they are all really important. What separates the leader from the manager is the self-awareness to understand the importance of moments, of interactions, because people won't remember what you said and they may not remember what you did, but they will always remember how you made them *feel*. Maya Angelou wrote that decades ago and it remains as true today.

As a leader you might come out with the best strategy ever or bring a new product to market in record time, and that's great, but people will only recall the interactions and the moments they had with you, and if they weren't so good, that is what they'll remember. There is real power in harnessing and capturing those moments and making them positive. All those moments and interactions create momentum, and you want that momentum to be positive, not negative.

In Antarctica, my performance review was conducted by a psychologist. It was totally honest, frank and fearless. Meeting privately with every person on the expedition team, she asked them about my performance as leader. She then took all that feedback and synthesised it.

When I sat down with the psychologist I asked her apprehensively, 'Well, what did they say? What did my people say about me?' 'That you are inspiring', she replied. 'What about me is inspiring?' I asked. Obviously it wasn't the fact that I chose to live in Antarctica for a year, I thought, because they're here with me.

What have I done to inspire them? 'Was it how I handled the plane crash?' She said no. 'Was it that I worked 16 hours a day all through summer, every day for four months?' No. 'Was it that I changed some of our policies so we have a lot more transparency around how our resources are allocated? Or maybe that Excel spreadsheet masterpiece I created for our rosters? What was it?'

She said, 'Well...Richard mentioned that his kid had a concert one day back in Australia and the next morning when you saw him you asked him if he'd phoned home to find out how Lachie's concert went. Martine said you knew the names of all 120 people on the station over summer *and* where they were from, and Ben said that one time he was on kitchen duty and he was mopping the floors, and he was still going at 9 o'clock at night, and you came in to get a cup of tea, and you just put a few chairs on the table to help him along—you didn't say anything, you just helped him out.'

And I thought, 'Really? That's all it was?' After a year of leadership? So I really didn't have to work those 16-hour days'. But it also brought home to me that it was the little moments, the small daily interactions they remembered and found inspiring. The moments that matter.

We expect our leaders to innovate and disrupt and create and be visionary. That's the big stuff, but it's the moments that matter that really make a difference to a team.

A leader understands the power of these moments. Every person you work with has their own social network at work. If you have a great interaction with them, they will go and tell all their networks. Equally, if you have a run-in with someone, you can guarantee it'll be around the office in ten minutes flat.

If you pile up consistently good moments, you build trust and confidence and people will act with commitment because they'll feel valued and respected, like an important part of the team.

If your moments are variable, and some mornings you come in and wish everyone a good morning, but the next day you forget or are a bit abrupt, then next day you are really friendly... people don't know what to expect, and that uncertainty breeds doubt, making them wary of you. They will act in accordance with your instructions, but they won't be sure how to approach you or where they stand.

If every time someone asks you, 'Can I have a word?' your response is an impatient sigh at the interruption, that behaviour builds mistrust and resignation, and you'll be met with resistance. People may do what you ask them to do, but probably only because they have to.

So what do these moments look like in the workplace? One of the most important moments is when someone approaches you and asks, 'Have you got a minute?' (and we know it's never a minute), how you respond to the interruption is a significant moment.

'Have you got a minute?'

For many years I asked myself, 'What's wrong with my time management?' Usually it was at the end of another long day in which I had been the first person in the office and was the last to leave, I'd missed lunch and had only ticked off two items on my to-do list. Or when I logged onto my email at night to catch up on the work I should have finished during the day.

It confounded me. I couldn't work out what the problem was. After 20 years spent in management roles in a range of complex and challenging settings, leading teams of up to 100 people at a time, I was entirely puzzled. I had attended numerous time management courses, had all the tools in place, yet still often felt swamped and ineffective.

It took my year in Antarctica to teach me it wasn't my time management that was the problem, it was my personal boundary management.

I arrived in Antarctica determined to be the best leader I could possibly be to my expeditioners. In my mind, this meant being available to my team and supporting them with clear direction, timely decision making, clarity of purpose and empathy.

So when they knocked on my bedroom door at all hours of the day and night seeking my input or decision on some issue or another—usually something important but not urgent—I took it in my stride. I was being available, supportive, a good leader.

Until the day they interrupted my breakfast one Sunday morning to have me sign a 'trip form' formally approving their plan to leave the station to do some sight-seeing (a safety policy). *Important but certainly not urgent.*

Then and there I realised that my approach was unsustainable. I simply could not be available, fully present and responsive to everyone, every hour of the day, for an entire year. I would burn out. I needed to manage my personal boundaries.

Personal boundaries separate us from other people and help define who we are and what we do. They apply in all aspects of life, whether at work, at home or in the community, and can:

- protect us
- minimise conflict
- promote healthy relationships.

The desire to respond immediately to enquiries and requests from other people is as natural as it is constant. For most of us it's about being supportive and encouraging. We want to be helpful and provide clear direction and advice.

However, when these interactions become interruptions (particularly at work) and our stress levels rise at the thought of the mountain of other work still needing our attention as we respond to each new request, they actually become a problem. We can become distracted and anxious, and it may become difficult to focus and be fully engaged in the conversation—to actually listen to, not just hear, what is being said.

How you handle this moment is important for two reasons.

Firstly, contemporary leadership is about creating more leaders, not more followers. Years ago, leaders could charge out the front and say, 'Follow me'. But if you try that now you will lose all your good people, especially your Gen Y and Gen Z staff, because more than any of their predecessors, these generations want to feel included, respected, valued. So the 'Have you got a minute?' interruption is a great moment to coach your colleagues about what the priority is, right now, in your job. Tell them: 'Not right now, as I need to get this briefing to the CEO's office by 3.00. Can you come back at 3.30?' Coach people about your work and they will respect the job you do—and your time.

Secondly, we all know when someone is not listening to us. We see it in their eyes that they have vagued out and are not really present. When someone asks you, 'Have you got a minute?' and you really don't but you say 'yes', naturally you will be distracted by the ton of work waiting for you. You will be thinking, I have to finish that sales report for tomorrow, and I need to write that agenda, and I have to set up that client meeting … and the person who interrupted you can see your mind is elsewhere. They will know you are not really listening and you may damage the relationship—all because you were trying to be helpful.

If you manage that boundary properly, however, you can build respect. If you ask the person to meet you at an arranged time, rather than discussing the matter spontaneously right now, they know they will have your full, undivided attention and can expect a considered response. This is what's best for *them*; it's not just about you. They may be surprised at first, but trust me, they will respect your honesty and probably envy your ability to manage boundaries effectively.

When I worked as a park ranger in regional Victoria I would often have the 'punters' (our stakeholders) approach me in the fish and chip shop or the supermarket to ask me what we were going to do 'about your rabbits getting out of the park and onto my land' or some other concern. My response was always the same. I told them they deserved my full attention and unfortunately I could not guarantee that in the breakfast cereal aisle of the IGA. I suggested they come in, or call me, when I was in the office on Monday, and then they would have my undivided attention.

This can be difficult in rural and regional areas, where everyone knows who you are and what you do. It's why in metropolitan areas many school teachers choose to live two or three suburbs away from the school they teach at! But you are not beholden to people who ask you about work when you are clearly not at work.

Turn it back on them so it becomes a positive for them. Explain why you can't be fully present, or even take notes, in this current setting and offer to follow up at a more appropriate time. They may not like it, but they will respect you for your ability to manage your personal boundaries.

PART III
Moments that matter and self-leadership

CHAPTER 6
Edge moments

Moments that matter can be so very simple. You notice that a colleague has missed morning tea and the cake you had to celebrate someone's birthday. So you set aside a slice with their name on it and put it in the fridge.

I was recently working with a multinational team of customer service people and I asked them to come up with some examples of moments that matter at work. In one anecdote a team leader was approached by a team member who thanked him on behalf of another staff member for pronouncing her friend's name correctly. When the person who offered this example admitted she wasn't even sure this was leadership, I replied, 'Absolutely it's leadership!' The fact that he'd taken the time to not only learn the staff member's name, but to pronounce it correctly, would have made her feel respected and valued, and like her boss really cared about her. This is big leadership in a small moment.

I remember my very first boss. I can't remember much of what he said to me or everything he did, but I remember how he inspired me. He made me believe I could do anything. He encouraged me to go for promotions and to take on new and different roles. I remember how competent and capable he made me feel.

The importance of these moments is that they all join together to create a perception and memory. Consistently great moments with someone will strengthen the relationship. That's what will stand out and that's why you're paid the big bucks.

Here I'll share a quick story about a time when I saw extraordinary leadership in a small moment. While in Antarctica we had a plane crash: a bolt had sheared off the landing gear of the plane and stranded four of my people 500 kilometres away from station.

The plane was okay, the fuselage was intact, but they had no landing gear, so they couldn't taxi, which meant they couldn't take off. So there they were, stranded hundreds of kilometres away. There were another 116 people on station at the time wondering how we were going to manage the rescue of these four people.

But the moment that stands out the most to me — the strongest, most vivid memory I have of this time — happened on the third day of the search and rescue. We were waiting for good weather so we could fly out there and retrieve them, and the search and rescue team (which included me, the weather forecasters and the pilots — six of us in total) hadn't had much sleep for three days. We'd dozed off and on but hadn't really slept, and this was day three. It was about 10 o'clock at night. We'd missed lunch and dinner, and we were hungry. The dining room is all packed away at 7 pm, but I said to the others, 'Look, we really need to eat. Let's just go to the kitchen and make ourselves some sandwiches.'

We walked into the kitchen ... and discovered that someone had plated up six dinners, covered them with cling film and stuck a Post-it note on each meal with our names on them.

Whoever had prepared these meals didn't know what each of us liked, of course. So we had a bit of everything: roast chicken, roast beef, roast lamb, a bit of roast pork (no vegetables!).

I just couldn't believe that someone had done this, someone had looked around and thought, 'What can I do to help? I know! I'll make sure the search and rescue team get fed.'

I found out who it was. It wasn't that hard. It was my diesel mechanic, and I went to her and said, 'Now that's amazing leadership!' She said, 'Oh no! I'm not the team leader. Gary is the team leader.'

I said, 'No, that's a title. Leadership isn't about titles, it's seeing something that needs to be done and doing it. You showed great leadership!'

I grant that in the context of that dramatic search and rescue mission it was only a small thing. But there were 116 people on station that day, and only one person thought creatively about how she could help.

That's leadership.

My expedition team didn't rate me as a strong leader because I delivered a program on time and on budget. Or because I maintained the safety and welfare of the 120 people at Davis Station over summer. Or because I managed the search and rescue following a plane crash. Equally, staff don't rate their manager as great because they deliver a product to market before the competition, or exceed sales targets, or manage dispersed teams across five international locations, or negotiate a tricky merger or acquisition. They figure this stuff is the leader's job. It's what they're paid to do.

In volunteer groups, people don't stick around and turn up for training and refresher work every week because their leader is a gun at raising funds for new equipment. Again, that's what they are expected to do.

What people remember and are inspired by, as I've said, are the moments. I call these 'edge moments' because they happen around the edges.

We all can bring to mind a boss or a teacher or a family member who made us feel great, just as most of us have a horror story or two about a boss who made us feel completely inadequate. We may not remember exactly what they said, but we sure do remember how they made us *feel*.

Of course, not every moment is an edge moment, a defining moment that will stay with us for a long time, so how do you identify one?

Incidentally, the term 'edge moments' came to me one day watching the Aurora Australis, or Southern Lights, in Antarctica. As any geophysicist can explain, the auroras are caused by solar wind (charged particles from the sun) hitting the geomagnetic field around the Earth. They happen at the south pole and north pole and are absolutely stunning. Beautiful curtains of green, or sometimes violet or red, but always stunning colours, dancing across the sky. Brief moments in time, they are nature's finest, most magical light show, like flashes of inspiring leadership.

Case study: Black Saturday bushfires

On my return from Antarctica I was part of the emergency response team during the Black Saturday bushfires in Victoria. It was the worst natural disaster in Australia for over 100 years: 173 people died and more than 7000 were displaced. Thousands more people were traumatised by the event; many of them still are. It was simply horrific.

Working in the Emergency Control Centre throughout the crisis I watched the extraordinary team response. Like many people there I was in a state of complete shock and felt quite overwhelmed at times.

One time I went into the kitchen to grab a coffee. We had an espresso machine that used a portafilter – the little thing with a handle that you put the ground beans into. I was waiting my turn when one of the planning officers ahead of me completely lost it. The person who had used the machine before him hadn't emptied out the ground coffee from the portafilter. It sent him into a huge rant about selfish, inconsiderate people. As I stood there trying to make sense of this – to understand why someone would choose that moment, on that day, to have a meltdown over a coffee machine – a senior manager walked in.

He assessed what was going on and quietly said to the guy, 'I know you're stressed and worried – we all are. We have no control over this fire, nothing we can do right now will round it up. I also know how annoying it is to have to empty someone else's coffee from the machine. But you're reacting to something you can control (the coffee) in the context of something totally out of your control (these fires), which makes perfect sense – we all want to control the things we can. But just imagine if all 100 people in this emergency centre did the same thing? If every one of us reacted the way you just have. What would happen to this emergency?'

I was gobsmacked, because I could not have done that. Right then, at that moment, I did not have the empathy to respond in that way. I would have just told the guy to pull his head in, and have made a difficult situation even worse.

In the context of this catastrophic event, the empathy and clear expectation shown by this manager was big leadership in a small moment. In the midst of the hell and chaos all around us, this leader acted quickly, recognising that the man needed to be heard but also needed to refocus. As I stood by and listened to the interaction I was in awe of this leader's capacity to stop and create that moment.

It took extraordinary leadership to assess instantly not just 'what' was going on but 'why'. Why was this guy reacting like this? He showed understanding and empathy and then, very importantly, he gave clear direction on his expectations as a leader.

Missed moments

As you can imagine Antarctica in winter is tough. That winter we were 18 strangers cooped up together for months of darkness with no way in or out. From May until August we couldn't even go outside unless it was absolutely necessary. It's intense.

My role as leader during this time was very much about inspiring people through the long, dark months. One of the ways I did this was to find reasons to celebrate.

Celebrating achievements—even small ones—breaks up the year and gives a sense of movement, of momentum, of going forward. Which is critical when there are no big projects, events or launches to work towards.

We celebrated 100 days without the server going down, we celebrated 50 days without a power blackout, we celebrated when we hit our water usage targets—I found any number of reasons to celebrate. It wasn't always with a party; in fact, usually I just wrote something on the whiteboard like, 'Great work diesel mechanics, 50 days without a power blackout', or I might say in our team meeting, 'Great effort everyone, 150 days without any LTIs [lost time injuries].' Or I might just say something privately. It depended on the person, because I knew that while some enjoyed public acknowledgment, others were embarrassed by it.

We also had a formal dinner every Saturday night to break up the week. By formal I mean the men might have a shave, the women might wear lipstick, and the tables had linen tablecloths—that's formal in Antarctica.

Each Saturday afternoon someone was rostered on to set the table and lay out the linen, glasses, cutlery. On this day it was my turn—because good leaders never ask their staff to do something they wouldn't do themselves, so I routinely rostered myself on to set the table.

I was busily setting away, lost in happy thoughts, occasionally looking out the window watching the iceberg out the front, when Rory walked in.

He said, 'Do you need a hand, Rach?'

'No thanks Rory, I'm good.'

'You sure? I'm not doing anything else right now?'

'Nope, thanks for the offer but I'm almost done.'

'I don't mind. I've got nothing else on.'

'*No!*' I said a little sharply. 'It's fine, I want to do it myself.'

As he walked off I realised I'd mishandled that moment. So then I overcompensated, and every time I saw Rory throughout the afternoon I'd jovially ask, 'Hey Rory, what are you up to?' or 'Hey Rory, how's your day been?' I felt horribly guilty that I had snapped at someone who was just trying to help me. I knew he would have been upset by my tone, because if it had been me I'd have felt the same way.

So the next time I saw him I said, 'Rory, I just wanted to say I'm sorry if I sounded a bit snappy before. It wasn't you. I actually really enjoy setting the table because it's easy stuff. It doesn't take much effort and it gives me a break from all the station leader stuff I do all day. So it's a little respite, time-out, that I find relaxing. But I should have explained that to you rather than snapping at you.'

He said, 'No worries at all Rach, I didn't even notice. But thanks.'

Initially, it was a missed moment because it could have been a chance to demystify myself and my role as a leader. Some people think leaders are different somehow, that they have different feelings or emotions. They don't. They are simply people who put up their hand to take on a leadership role—they have the same feelings as anyone else. This moment would have been a perfect time to explain to Rory that my role leading people 24/7 can sometimes get intense, and exhausting, so the opportunity to vague out and do something as mind-numbingly simple as putting glasses on a table was actually relaxing, and cathartic. But I missed the moment. And while I did eventually follow up with Rory, it would have been much better to have explained myself in the moment.

No one expects leaders to get it right all the time—we're only human and don't have superpowers—but if we quickly recognise our mistake, reflect on it and follow up, the opportunity might not be missed after all.

How to make the most of edge moments

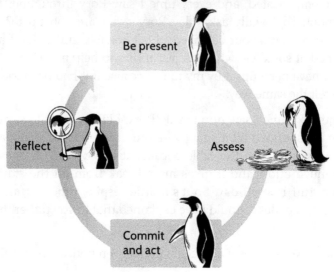

Edge moments are about showing big leadership in small moments. They're about knowing what to do in a given situation. And importantly, they're about knowing what *not* to do.

1. BE PRESENT

'Being present' means maintaining two views at once—the ground-level view and the helicopter view. The ground-level view focuses on the behaviours, the complaints, the niggling differences in interpersonal relationships. The helicopter view sees the bigger picture and asks, what's really going on here? The helicopter view takes in the team, the company, the macroeconomic environment you operate in.

Incidentally, in most parts of the world where bushfires are a threat, one of the most reliable ways we have of spotting a fire is to have a human being standing on top of a tower in the forest scanning the horizon for smoke. Even with drones and satellite technology, the most reliable warning system is still an alert set of eyes.

Leaders need both views. They need a nuanced understanding of the individuals in their team, but equally, they need an overall view of the factors that impact their team. They need to scan the horizon looking for smoke.

2. ASSESS

When someone confronts you with a problem they need you to solve, or an issue they want your input on, or a decision they want you to make, how do you decide how to respond?

To assess the moment and decide how to proceed, recall the Step In, Step Back model: take a few seconds and ask yourself the two questions: (1) Does it impact on the team's values? and (2) How many people does it affect? Your answers will determine your actions: Step Back, Defuse, Step In or Escalate.

Use the team values as the navigation point. No matter what these values are—whether integrity, teamwork, loyalty, respect, collaboration or something quite different—you have already decided that these are the most important guiding principles for your team. They are what you hold dear and what you believe will make you successful. They are also what you navigate towards whenever you're in doubt.

3. COMMIT AND ACT

Once you have made your assessment the next step is to commit to it and act on it. This needs to be done with conviction and humility and in a timely manner. Communicate why you're dealing with the issue in this way, or explain why you have determined not to act on it.

In Antarctica one of my best expeditioners injured himself while dancing on a coffee table. It was a silly thing to do and he knew it. Unfortunately for him, word of his antics soon got out.

I happened to be in the kitchen the morning after the table dancing incident when the phone rang. It was our neighbours at Mawson Station, 1500 kilometres away.

Mawson: 'So how is Ben?'

Me: 'Um, what do you mean how's Ben? What's happened?'

Mawson: 'Well, he was dancing on a coffee table last night and fell off and cracked some ribs.'

What? The fact that I had found out about the incident via another station told me I needed to act fast. So I called Ben into my office. Together, we agreed that his punishment would be to complete a 500-piece jigsaw puzzle on that table. The reason we decided on this course was twofold. I needed to address the poor behaviour, but as this was one of my very best expeditioners I wanted to do it without escalating the issue. After almost eight months of exemplary service, this was his first misstep, so there was really no call to crucify him. But equally, I couldn't play favourites and turn a blind eye completely. That would be unfair to the rest of the team.

By having him complete the jigsaw puzzle in the lounge room I was sending a very public message that I had spoken to him and reproved him. As one of the leaders in the group he was hugely embarrassed by his behaviour and he wanted to set a better example. The jigsaw was a symbolic way for him to acknowledge to his colleagues that he had acted irresponsibly. Importantly, it was his choice. It was also quite funny. No one had yet completed a jigsaw puzzle, so it was perhaps a fitting punishment for a decidedly unusual crime.

4. REFLECT

Self-awareness is one of the hallmarks of a great leader. It demonstrates a capacity to honestly evaluate your own actions, beliefs and impact on others. But it is a quality that eludes many people. Our understanding of ourselves and our world is limited. It is rare that we take the time to step back from our thoughts and reflect on the reality of the situations we are in and the role we play in creating that reality.

As leaders we need to reflect on this every day: How did I handle that situation? Did someone respond very differently from how I imagined they would, and if so what role did I play in that? Take a few minutes every day to reflect on how you handled situations and identify what worked and what didn't.

CHAPTER 7
Self-awareness and self-leadership

Recent research into the common traits of hundreds of highly successful leaders has shown that the number one quality that enabled those leaders to achieve greatness was self-awareness. Sure, they have many other important traits, but the one quality that is found in every great leader is the ability to look at themselves critically and to see themselves as others see them.

Self-awareness includes the ability to look at how you influence events. How did my words and my actions impact that situation? What role did I play? It's the ability to look down from the balcony and watch yourself, and critically analyse your actions. How did I handle that? Could I have done something better? What did I do really well and can I do that again?

If your self-awareness is poor you'll be surprised by how people react to the things you do and say, and you'll struggle to get people to see things from your perspective. The good news is you can build your self-awareness. There are four main ways you can do this. The first is through reflection—thinking back on how you handled a situation or made a decision, and learning from that.

The second way is to seek out frank and fearless advice from someone you trust. Run it by them and see what they have to offer. The third way is to develop a professional relationship with a mentor, someone who can guide you and provide feedback and advice. The fourth approach to consider is psychometric testing. There are dozens of these tests that can offer insights into your thinking and communication preferences and styles.

Journaling

One of the best ways to reflect on your leadership is through journaling. The purpose of a journal is to capture, more or less in real time, your thoughts, decisions, actions and immediate responses. You record the thoughts as they occur to you, rather than aiming for well-turned prose.

The idea is that the process of writing about them helps you to understand the things that happened and to grow. Don't filter your thoughts in your journal and don't sanitise them. Always handwrite your journal, because when we type, we tend to self-correct and that gets in the way of the natural flow. Just record the stream of your thoughts, then use that to look back and see how you handled each situation, and that will inform your future practice.

A journal is a great learning tool. You can later reflect on everything you do and every time you make a decision. This creates a loop in which you learn, act, reflect; learn, act, reflect; and learn again. And this builds leadership capability.

Case study: Journaling on slushy duty

Football was at the core of one of the greatest changes in my leadership style.

It all started with my being rostered on as the on-duty 'slushy'. The kitchen assistant, or slushy, helps the chef prepare the meals for the day. You peel potatoes, chop onions or whatever else the chef needs help with. Some people really look forward to their shift as slushy because it provides a welcome respite from critical but mundane winter tasks such as stocktakes. Others perform the role grudgingly because it's a compulsory requirement, but they really don't enjoy being in the kitchen.

As a sweetener, you get to choose what music is played in the living quarters. The music is also transmitted throughout the station and picked up on the radio of each vehicle. So the entire community gets to enjoy whatever songs the slushy chooses to play.

One day over winter a couple of people decided they would prefer to listen to a live broadcast of the AFL than music while on slushy duty. I didn't pay much attention to this until a small contingent came to me to complain that the policy was 'whoever is on slushy picks the *music*, not footy'. They didn't want to hear sport broadcast over the station's radio station. The next day a rival delegation insisted that the policy was 'slushy's choice'. Whether that choice was music or sport was beside the point, in their opinion.

My predicament as leader was that there actually was *no policy*. It was simply a cultural tradition that had evolved over time and there was never a clear, specific protocol for what should or should not be played over the radio. I was stumped, at a loss as to how to manage this one.

So I did what I do best. I consulted. I canvassed every single person on station and asked, 'What do *you* think we should do?'

Suddenly it became the biggest issue to hit Antarctica in 58 years of Australian expeditions! Everyone was talking about it, and I mean *everyone*.

I struggled to understand why this was such a critical issue. As I wrote in my journal each night, reflecting on the day's events and my performance as leader, I knew I was missing something but couldn't grasp what it was. Why was this so important? What had happened?

(continued)

Case study: Journaling on slushy duty *(cont'd)*

Then the penny dropped. What had happened was *me*. The reason everyone was talking about it was because I had asked every person for their opinion. By seeking input from the entire community, I had escalated the issue to the point where people who had previously been unaware of it, or indifferent to it, suddenly had a strong opinion on it!

By adopting my usual democratic style, I had turned this straightforward issue into a big, hairy monster. In hindsight I should have realised I would never get a consensus decision from the team. I already had one group totally opposed to listening to the footy and another group just as strongly supporting the slushy's freedom of choice. Common sense should have told me I'd have to make the call myself.

The only way I came to understand what had happened was by reflecting on it in my journal. By writing down what had happened I was able to look back and realise, 'That was me. I did that'. If I hadn't worked it through in my journal I might easily have written the incident off as a case of cabin fever. I might have assumed, incorrectly, that the reason it had become such an issue was because we were all going slightly bonkers. I would have attributed the escalation to the fact that people were under intense interpersonal pressure, rather than recognising the real issue, which was that I hadn't adjusted my decision-making style to the situation.

Sometimes it's best to be consultative and democratic; sometimes you need to recognise you're being paid to make a decision and just make it; and at other times it's best to adopt a laissez faire style, step back and let your team sort it out for themselves.

The most important skill for any leader is developing the judgement and experience to know when to adopt a particular style. In the end I did make the decision myself. I decided that anyone who didn't want to listen to the footy on the radio should just turn their own radio off.

A blindingly brilliant decision, if I do say so myself!

Three domains of leadership

Self-leadership and self-awareness impact on the rest of your leadership ability.

There are three main domains of leadership:

1. **Self-leadership**—your self-awareness, your ability to understand how you impact others, and your ability to step back and reflect on how you handled a situation.

2. **Business leadership**—understanding the market you're operating in, understanding the macroeconomic environment, your customers, your shareholders or stakeholders, and why you're in the business you're in; your business acumen.

3. **Team leadership**—the ability to lead, inspire and motivate others, harnessing those skills to deliver great performance.

Each of these domains is critical for business success, but they can't operate in isolation—you actually need to be across all three. Focus on two and forget the third and you are doomed to failure.

GREAT SELF-LEADERSHIP AND BUSINESS LEADERSHIP BUT NO TEAM LEADERSHIP

For example, perhaps you've got great self-leadership and self-awareness, you know your strengths and your weaknesses, and you're also well across your business and understand the environment you operate in. But if you're forgetting about the other team members, then you'll tend to find that most of the work ends up gravitating to you. Without the ability to lead your team and have them deliver the work for you, you will burn out. You will be putting so much energy and effort into the business that others will step back. You need to be spending more time in bringing your people along with you.

GREAT TEAM LEADERSHIP AND GREAT SELF-LEADERSHIP BUT NO BUSINESS LEADERSHIP

Perhaps, instead, you're focusing all your effort on others and building a great team, inspiring and motivating them, and you also have terrific self-awareness. The result will be a great, fun working environment, but nothing will get done, and the business will suffer. So, while everyone will enjoy coming to work, soon they may not have work to come to! You really need to focus on the business as well.

GREAT TEAM LEADERSHIP AND BUSINESS LEADERSHIP BUT NO SELF-LEADERSHIP

Leaders who spend a lot of time and energy focusing on their teams and team performance, and an equal amount of energy on growing the business, but don't dedicate any time to developing their own self-leadership and self-awareness, are often identified by the following symptoms:

1. They attribute any problems that occur to other people's shortcomings, rather than their own.

2. They have no sense of how their actions, words, mood and body language affect the people around them.

3. They haven't yet worked on their own personal stuff—their lifestyle choices and decisions—so any shortcomings or failings tend to impact the team around them. For example, a lack of confidence may lead to micro-management.

4. They make decisions based almost exclusively on their own perspective and needs. They never engage their team in important decisions.

5. They don't ask for feedback from others, because they know they are doing a great job.

6. They get upset when someone questions what they do. They often interpret a robust discussion about an issue as a personal affront.

7. They have yet to find deep personal fulfilment and happiness, and this affects how they relate to other people.

8. All their actions and decisions are based on their own ego rather than on what is in the best interests of the team or organisation.

9. They worry about how things will affect them, but not others. You will find this particularly when there is change.

10. They have difficulty praising the great work that others do, often feeling this minimises their own work and efforts.

That's a cracker of a list, isn't it? And somewhere in the world there is someone who ticks all of these boxes. You might even know them.

At the other end of the spectrum are those rare individuals who are entirely self-aware and who totally understand how they impact the people around them. Most of us fall somewhere in the middle.

PART IV
No triangles in action

CHAPTER 8
Implementing no triangles

Integrity is critical to a team's success, and the lack of it unquestionably leads to poor performance. Teams and organisations need simple ways to encourage the right behaviours and the tools to call out behaviours that are counterproductive. One simple teamwork tool can increase staff productivity by up to 40 per cent.

Though the impact of this behaviour varies across industries, what is resoundingly true across all businesses is that spending time in 'triangle' conversations is both time-consuming and exhausting, especially for leaders.

Leaders should be allocating their time to the actions that have the most impact on the business's bottom line, and right at the top of this list is retaining talent. That means spending time with your best performers and making sure their contribution is valued. Any leader who is caught up in the repetitive loop of 'triangle' conversations simply won't have the time or energy to acknowledge their best contributors.

Leaders lose their way when they attach more importance to team harmony than integrity and respect. This is when leaders spend their time listening to staff vent or complain about their colleagues, with no real determination to solve the problem. These leaders just want to keep the peace, which is dangerous.

My expedition team in Antarctica was incredibly diverse across many measures, including age, gender, religion, profession and cultural background, so it was unrealistic to imagine we would all live together for an entire year as best friends. It simply wouldn't happen, and I didn't expect it to. Rather, as leader, my expectation was we would always treat each other with integrity and respect.

When a team focuses on harmony as its main goal, several things happen.

Firstly, any bullying or harassment will persist; it just goes underground. People won't raise the issue because they don't want to be the person who rocks the harmony boat. So they keep quiet. The job of the leader is to deal with these issues as and when they arise. Being seen to manage the issues, rather than sweep them under the carpet for the sake of team unity, is critical.

Secondly, when you focus on harmony and minimise any differences, you are unlikely to generate innovation. You cannot innovate when everyone is focused on agreeing! People won't air a different opinion or a conflicting view, or engage in robust debate, because, again, they don't want to upset the harmonious balance. The role of a leader in this situation is to canvass different ideas and encourage discussion of all options—in other words, find the best outcome or solution from a wide range of diverse people with different levels of experience.

Thirdly, and most importantly, when a team focuses on harmony, to the exclusion of all else, people can get hurt, both physically or mentally, which exposes the business to additional risk. People turn a blind eye to someone acting unsafely, for example not following the correct safety protocols, because they don't want to upset the status quo. They want to keep the peace.

Research shows that in workplaces where safety is paramount (for example, in mining, resources, utilities, manufacturing and construction) the most critical inhibitor to people stepping in to put a stop to unsafe activities is the need to feel included. If for any reason a person feels excluded or not part of the team, they will not get involved in safety leadership. This happens wherever a culture of harmony and homogeneity prevails over a culture of integrity and respect. In these workplaces especially, people need to feel included and respected. Not loved, just respected. And the leader sets the tone by stepping in and managing the issue, every time.

Similarly, if the focus is on a happy and harmonious team, where everything is great, people are less likely to admit to any unhappiness. If everyone else feels great, then they best keep quiet about not feeling the same way.

Lastly, people often walk away from unethical behaviour. Even if they know the behaviour is wrong, and will end up significantly damaging the business, they choose to ignore it because they believe that keeping the peace is the greater good. In recent history many financial institutions around the world have collapsed under the weight of the unethical behaviour of a small group of staff. It's certain that other people in the business were aware of what was going on, but instead of intervening or reporting the behaviour, they chose to look away—with devastating consequences.

A team built on harmony alone is an illusion that will crumble under pressure.

A few years back a company I worked for organised all my travel and accommodation requirements for a series of their events. One day they made a significant error, booking me to speak at two different events, 1200 kilometres apart, within 12 hours. A robust team would have identified the mistake and called a few people into a room to brainstorm possible solutions. But this team emphasised a culture of harmony over one of respect (that is, dealing with issues), which meant the young staffer who'd made the mistake rang me from a mobile phone in the car park in tears, trying to convey the error without any colleagues finding out. This behaviour could in part be attributed to pride and wanting to do a great job, but, knowing the team as well as I did, I knew the bigger issue was a fear of admitting they'd made a mistake, thereby upsetting the team dynamic.

My Antarctic team were fantastic in a crisis. When we had to manage the search and rescue following the plane crash, the team worked incredibly well under pressure. Given that we were to be together for over a year, with no way to get away from each other, I recognised from the start how important it was to build a resilient culture where people would speak up and address issues directly and not let them fester.

My role as leader was to model that behaviour, and it started with the principle of *no triangles*. I was always willing to step in and resolve an issue between staff—but only after they had first tried to sort it out for themselves. And I simply couldn't be seen, or heard, complaining about one of the team or about head office, even if only letting off steam, because such behaviour is disrespectful and the leader sets the tone for the rest of the team.

In Antarctica we created a strong, adaptable and high-performing team, not because we all loved each other, but because our culture of integrity and respect ensured we learned to respect each other's contribution to the team.

How to introduce the principle of no triangles

It would be fantastic to be able to stand up at a staff meeting and say, 'Okay, from today we're having *no triangles* in our workplace', and have it just happen. But like all organisational change, people first need to understand what it is, why they're being asked to change their behaviour and what life will look like if they're successful.

This is especially important with volunteer groups that depend on people donating their time and energy. Unless *no triangles* is introduced properly it may be perceived as a criticism or a cop-out by the leaders, so explaining why you're introducing the principle is critical.

My advice is to start with your immediate team. If you're not the team leader, take your team leader aside and explain what you see happening, its impacts and what can be done about it. Then champion it yourself. Model the behaviour.

Modelling the behaviour is all about leading from where you are, not relying on being in a position of power. The moment you feel the urge to create a triangle, take a deep breath and resist it. Gather the courage to have a direct conversation with the person involved. Even if it doesn't go exactly as planned, that person will likely respect you for trying.

When someone comes to you to create a triangle, look them in the eye and ask, 'Have you spoken to them about it yet?' Sometimes they will have tried and been unsuccessful. Help them work out what went wrong and encourage them to go back and try again. But don't get involved in it yourself, unless it's your role.

Steps to implementation

1. **Provide the why.** Why is *no triangles* so important to your team. Make it clear that we value direct feedback, we value integrity and honest conversations. You're not implying there's a huge issue with triangles in your team (unless that is in fact the case); rather, you're saying that 'as a team we are good, but through the practice of *no triangles* we can be great.'

2. **Provide the what.** Explain what 'direct conversations' means and, importantly, provide the tools to have the difficult conversation.

3. **Provide the how.** Explain how we all need to put our hand up and commit to the behaviour. Then we must all be rock solid and consistent in our commitment. Change takes time too, so remember to support each other along the way.

Barriers to implementing no triangles

During my research for this book I discovered that the number one barrier to implementing *no triangles*, the thing that holds us back more than anything else, is overwhelmingly a lack of confidence in our ability to effectively conduct that conversation in a respectful way in order to achieve the outcome we want.

In a *Harvard Business Review* article, 'What's Worse than a Difficult Conversation? Avoiding One', Deborah Rowland suggests one of the main reasons we avoid difficult conversations is not that we're afraid of upsetting the other person; it's our own unconscious anxiety about not being able to handle the conversation well. 'Overcoming these anxieties and having the tough conversations anyway is one of a top leader's most difficult challenges — critically needed, yet chronically hard to do.'

While I agree they are critically needed, I don't accept that they are 'chronically hard to do'. Yes, they can be uncomfortable and challenging, but I believe that with the right preparation and attitude you can conduct these conversations with great confidence. It's a learned skill — it takes practice. There are dozens of courses on offer and many books have been written on the topic. To simplify things for the teams I work with I have created a checklist, '10 steps for difficult conversations' (see appendix II).

The list had its origins in Antarctica. One day one of the guys came and shared with me that Jason had upset him by something he'd said at the dinner table.

'Well, what did Jason say when you spoke to him about it', I asked him.

'Oh, I didn't', he replied.

'Okay', I said. 'You need to speak to him about it, not me.' And I went through some of the initial steps with him — things like picking the right time of day to have the conversation, focusing on the facts and data, taking out the emotion, showing empathy and trying to predict where the conversation might go next.

'Great!' and off he went.

The next day he came back and said, 'Oh, I told Jason about that issue'.

'So how did it go?'

'Well, actually I sent him an email ...'

No, never! You never *ever* conduct these conversations via email. Email has no tone. It's impersonal, one-way and definitely not the tool to use in this sort of context.

You need to have the conversation face to face. So I went through it again, offering much the same guidelines: pick the right time of day, deal with the facts, show some empathy …

He came back to me later that week. He said, 'I had the conversation with Jason'. 'So how did it go?', I asked. 'Well, I waited till he'd had a few beers!', he replied.

Sigh.

But the incident got me thinking that if I could come up with a structured approach to these conversations and we went about it as we do anything we need to practise, any training program we need to take on, and just do it, then surely the more we practise, the better we will get at it.

A few years ago I formulated a concept I called the LADAR, representing our Language Radar (see figure 2). The idea was that certain words would *ping* on our LADAR when we heard them, much like an object pings on a radar or sonar system.

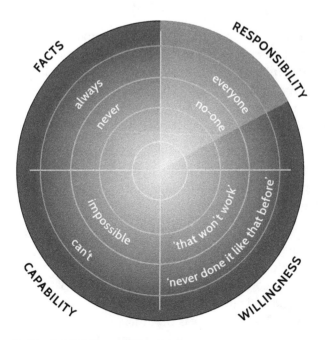

Figure 2: the LADAR—a nifty tool

I was inspired to coin the term LADAR because at Davis Station we have a piece of scientific equipment called a LIDAR, a light imaging, detecting and ranging system, which shoots a green laser beam into the stratosphere. The scientists use it to study the temperature and movement of air in the stratosphere, so it plays an important role in climate science.

On my radar were certain words that I didn't want to use, and if someone else used them I had a way to challenge their use of the word. They began with *absolute* and *unconditional* terms such as 'everyone' and 'no-one'. If someone comes up to you and says, 'Oh, everyone thought that was a bad idea', that should *ping* your LADAR, so challenge it. Ask them, 'Everyone? Really? So if I were to ask any member of the team, they would be of exactly the same opinion? Really? everyone? It's not everyone, it's you'.

Total unanimity is very unusual, so it's rarely everyone and it's rarely no-one. Listen out for those words, because often they indicate a person is avoiding taking direct responsibility for an issue. And avoid using them yourself!

Words such as 'unfinished', 'not ready' and 'unsure' can indicate a barrier around their willingness. There's a reason why a person is reluctant to fully commit. You need to ask a few questions: Why do they say they are not ready? What is standing between them and committing to the idea? Why are they saying it's not quite finished when you know it's ready to go? Just chip in and ask a few questions.

In the third sector are absolutes such as 'impossible' and 'can't'. They can often be a signal of doubt in the user's own capabilities to complete the task, so they may need mentoring or training or more development, or just a bit more experience.

The last quadrant is my favourite. Here you'll find absolutes like 'always' and 'never', which are in fact rarely accurate. This one is particularly critical when you're having a performance management conversation. You accuse someone of 'always' being late for work, and almost before the word leaves your mouth they reply, 'Well, yesterday I was 30 minutes early'. Your argument is blown out of the water, and the conversation will be difficult to recover from there. I've seen how easily these conversations turn into really emotional, 'he said, she said' exchanges once this happens. You need to stick to facts and data.

You might say, for example, 'On the last three Mondays, you've arrived at 9.30. You're due to start at 9 o'clock. We talked about this a month ago, and you said there was no barrier to your getting here on time, yet you're still turning up late.' It's much harder to argue with facts and data than it is to debate absolutes such as *always, never, everyone* and *no one*.

So listen out for words like these when you're communicating with someone, and make sure you don't use them yourself.

Good triangles

Of course, as with all principles, there are grey areas around the edges as well as obvious exceptions. It's totally okay to go straight to the boss or HR to let them know about behaviour that is immoral, unethical or illegal, or in other ways clearly violates your organisation's values. That's what managers, leaders and HR people are there for. Trust me, execs and HR people would be delighted if the only personal issues they had to deal with were those that clearly needed to be escalated!

Also, sometimes you will have had the difficult conversation and still made no progress. At times like this it's good to agree to have a mediator involved. It could be your boss, or someone from HR or even someone from outside the organisation. The key thing here is that you've tried to resolve it between yourselves first.

My research shows it generally takes about two months to embed *no triangles* in an existing culture, but eventually it will become 'how we work around here'.

That's the simple power of *no triangles*. When every member of the team has made the commitment to *no triangles*, it takes away the scariness of the conversation. Because it's just how we work around here.

Case study: Atlassian

Many of us have experienced the 'brilliant jerk' – the obnoxious individual who lacks self-awareness but is excellent at their technical work. They are an absolute pain to work with, yet the company keeps them on because they close extraordinary deals, or exceed sales targets, or develop innovative software or games. The senior leadership turn a blind eye to the poor behaviour because this individual delivers results. But this is no longer true of Australian enterprise software company Atlassian.

Atlassian develops products for software developers, project managers and content managers. The company has just completed a 12-month trial and is now rolling out a new performance review framework. This framework won't focus only on the expectations of their roles – the KPIs that elevate the brilliant jerk; it will also include two other assessment pillars: the contribution the individual makes to their team, and their demonstration of company values. Each of the assessment areas is weighted equally to determine a performance rating.

The 'contribution to the team' assessment measures, among other things, how far employees go to elevate their teammates' impact and overall team performance, and their efforts to foster an environment of trust and belonging.

For 'demonstration of values' employees are rated against the company's five key values. The 'expectation of role' metrics have also been expanded to encompass the employee's efforts to identify gaps in plans, to course-correct projects and to inspire others to greater levels of performance.

Assessing the employee in all three areas ensures no brilliant jerks are given a high rating.

CHAPTER 9
Research results and feedback

Over the past 14 years I have worked with hundreds of teams that
have implemented *no triangles* in their culture. I recently surveyed
200 of these teams to collect feedback on how the process was
working out, what could be improved and what benefits they
could attribute directly to the practice of *no triangles*.

After processing the survey results, my team and I then conducted
follow-up phone calls with respondents who offered to provide
more detailed feedback.

Several common themes were identified across the group, as well
as some ideas for improvement and ongoing engagement.

How did no triangles work for you?

Several teams noted that the tool was particularly useful in
addressing existing issues and cultural concerns, and that it was
even more powerful once it became embedded in the culture and
part of the language:

'Staff are engaged in the process and are using the language; I
regularly hear the term *no triangles*.'

'*No triangles* has allowed us to bring issues to the surface and
address them.'

'Back in 2016 we had quite a toxic culture, with high staff turnover. Since implementing *no triangles* I have seen marked improvements, which I can only attribute to the new practice.'

'It works incredibly well when it becomes business as usual and not just something we raise on planning days. It becomes part of the daily conversation.'

'*No triangles* caught fire in our organisation. I implemented it with my managers. The CEO heard about it and wants it rolled out throughout the organisation.'

No triangles provides a framework for people to have difficult conversations and has been demonstrated to improve ability, confidence and resilience:

'Now that the staff are talking directly to one another they are also working out how to help one another. Consequently there's been a noticeable increase in confidence across the organisation.'

'It has allowed us to interact professionally and have the courage to hold the difficult conversations, because it's now how we operate around here.'

'When I was in a triangles situation I found I was brave enough to call it out. The other person was a bit stumped by my honesty, but it made life easier for me in the long run.'

It reduces barriers and confusion, focusing on the behaviour rather than the person:

'It allows us to extract the emotion from the feedback, encouraging constructive conversation and forward momentum.'

'It has helped give people a better understanding of each other and what they and the organisation are about.'

'It allows for immediate feedback, which helps take the emotion and angst out of the conversation.'

No triangles isn't industry specific. It is a simple concept and relatable at all levels:

'I work in a hospital where we use *no triangles*. Though it's a simple concept, the principles behind it are very important. I have never *not* seen a lightbulb moment from people when they start using it.'

'The expressions themselves – *respect trumps harmony, bacon wars* and *no triangles* – are really handy and keep it memorable.'

'Keeping it simple makes it memorable. *No triangles* and *respect trumps harmony* are simple concepts that don't feel contrived.'

'It isn't management-speak, and it's easily absorbed. It applies in any sector or industry.'

How can you improve no triangles?

One survey respondent was managing several volunteer fire and rescue brigades. The work involved high levels of conflict so they implemented the tool very slowly. They also developed a set of visual aids to display around the station as a reminder.

In one case, the process was unsuccessful because the team felt it was foisted on them. A lack of communication around why *no triangles* was being implemented meant some of the team perceived it as a way for managers to hide behind the process:

'We tried the strategy and had the conversation, but when it still couldn't be resolved we took it back to our manager. She just told us to go back and try again.'

'We implemented *no triangles* but we soon worked out that it was our managers who were the worst offenders. They are not walking the walk and just pay lip service to it.'

To successfully implement this tool, leaders need to model the behaviour and provide a compelling case for why *no triangles* is being used, as well as the tools, including coaching, where needed:

'We understood the concept but didn't know how to actually have the conversation.'

'Some of our team really dislike conflict and are resistant to a direct conversation because it feels like conflict to them.'

'We needed more guidance around active listening and resilience, and not becoming defensive.'

'Some case studies would be really useful, as some of my team found it hard to conceptualise what it means and how to go about having the conversation.'

No triangles as a recruitment tool

Culture fit is the glue that holds an organisation together, which is why recruiting the right people to a team is so important. Before recruitment starts, it is essential for an organisation to be able to define and articulate its culture—its values, goals and practices—then use this understanding in the hiring process.

Several organisations that have implemented *no triangles* and *respect trumps harmony* within their organisation have identified the need to ensure they are recruiting the right people—that is, that the new hire will be able to reflect and adapt to the core beliefs, attitudes and behaviours within the organisation.

The following are examples of questions that will assist in assessing culture fit:

- What type of culture do you thrive in? (Does the response align with your organisational culture?)

- What values are you drawn to and what's your ideal workplace?

- Why do you want to work here?

- Tell me about the most stressful situation you have faced at work. What happened? How did you handle it?

- What, in your opinion, are the key ingredients in maintaining successful business relationships?

- Describe a situation in which your colleagues disagreed with your ideas. What did you do?

- Describe a time when you worked with or for an organisation where you felt the absence of a strong culture fit. Why was it a bad fit?

There are many benefits to recruiting the right people for your organisation. Ensuring that your people flourish, both in their professional roles and socially, drives productivity and success and ultimately saves you time and money.

Supporting existing wellbeing and learning and development programs

No triangles also feeds into existing values and the Code of Conduct and other existing wellbeing and learning and development programs:

> 'We also use the Instant Feedback model. That and *no triangles* complement each other.'

> 'We discussed the approach at a team planning day. In particular, we set out to identify the non-negotiables for the team: these included no incivility, *no triangles* and no drama.'

> 'We use the Banaam principle, which is based on Indigenous cultural principles, and *no triangles* feeds directly into and complements this framework.'

> '*No triangles* was a catalyst in making other strategies work as well as they have within the organisation.'

Dispute resolution and employee relations

No triangles and *respect trumps harmony* are preventative strategies that can reduce the incidence of miscommunication, misunderstanding and, in many cases, bullying in the workplace. They can also be used as an intervention strategy where there are issues that have escalated. Managers have a crucial role in supporting their staff, guiding them towards the necessary conversations and managing situations at the lowest level possible.

Human resources staff are also well placed to use and encourage the use of these tools—for example, where there are allegations of bullying and harassment, or where poor relationships have become so toxic they lead to the diagnosis of a medical condition. Having these conversations as early as possible results in fewer formal investigations and better outcomes for staff affected.

Feedback from organisations on this topic is often more complex:

> 'When I came to the role there were significant leadership problems. Two leaders had had a nervous breakdown. It was messy; there was discontent and high staff turnover. Getting staff to use the *no triangles* strategy brought the issues to the surface, so they could be dealt with.'

> 'As a workplace investigator I remind people of the issues of confidentiality, values and the code of conduct, and that talking to other people creates more problems by making these triangles. I will use the strategy and implement it as part of the solution in my investigations. For example, staff will be encouraged to go back to all those they have spoken to about the issue and tell them it is now resolved and they are happy with the outcome.'

Embedding it in the culture

Our research and feedback indicates that *no triangles* has been most successful when senior leaders and management have taken on a significant role in supporting the strategy and embedding it in the culture and values of the organisation:

> '*No triangles* has been critical in cultural development. The Principal trained all staff leaders, who then ensured the ideas filtered down to staff pods.'

> 'I have five direct reports and make it my business to understand them, their strengths and their weaknesses. As a leader I need to understand the strategy and then convey that to the next level of leadership.'

Consistent and ongoing messaging from the leadership demonstrates commitment within an organisation. It has been shown that where staff feel they can be guided and coached by their managers and supported through the process, they are more likely to not only to use the strategy but to see it as a tool that will work. This in turn builds confidence, and increases open and transparent communication within teams:

> 'Staff are very engaged and are using the language. I hear the term *no triangles* regularly.'

> 'I have two managers reporting to me. We all undertook to support staff where there were issues and to coach them and guide them through their discussions.'

> 'I can see that staff are now really embracing the strategy. Staff are coming to me to ask for advice on how to have this conversation. I've been very supportive of this and will coach them through the process.'

Practically, organisations have been implementing *no triangles* through:

- inclusion in regular team meetings
- inclusion as an agenda item at planning days
- use of visual aids
- coaching and mentoring sessions with staff.

CHAPTER 10
Research evidence and conclusions

In writing this book, I surveyed 200 teams that have implemented *no triangles* to quantify the benefits. The teams ranged across Fortune 500 companies, the public sector, community groups and not-for-profit organisations. The survey asked eight questions to establish exactly what impact the use of this tool had on individuals and teams.

The idea was to try to translate into reliable data what the anecdotal evidence had already shown. The results were unequivocal and to me, astounding. I knew there would be positive benefits, but I underestimated just how much impact *no triangles* would have on relationships and results.

Without exception, every one of the 200 teams that were surveyed identified improvements in their team dynamics and performance that directly correlated with the implementation of a *no triangles* culture.

Morale, decision making, productivity, accountability and, most importantly, respect, all showed a significant improvement.

1. Implementing no triangles saves time and increases productivity

How much time do you think you have freed up?

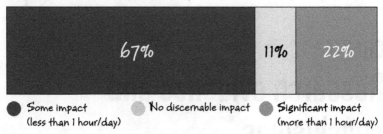

| 67% | 11% | 22% |

● Some impact
(less than 1 hour/day)
● No discernable impact
● Significant impact
(more than 1 hour/day)

Implementing no triangles in your culture will significantly increase team productivity.

No triangles frees up time, with 89 per cent of respondents replying they had more time in their day once these conversations stopped. A large group (22 per cent) replied they had freed up more than one hour every day. Imagine what you could do with an extra five hours a week?

The time saved by not engaging in distracting, and ultimately futile, conversations can be directed towards activities that add value to your team or business.

For leaders, the research points overwhelmingly to the importance of spending time recognising and supporting their talented people and acknowledging their work or behaviour. Becoming caught up in triangle conversations is both exhausting and counterproductive, because they then don't have the time or energy to spend with their good people. It's especially important in volunteer groups that the leaders acknowledge, mentor and spend time with their great people.

One survey respondent said: 'When I came into my role there were three interlinked projects being managed separately instead of working together. After being introduced to *no triangles* and *the bacon war,* the team became more collaborative, with improved productivity and financial savings.'

In the survey 89 per cent of respondents said implementing *no triangles* had improved their productivity by freeing up time to get on with their more important work.

Besides gaining time, adopting a culture of *no triangles* frees up personal energy. The energy spent on these redundant conversations can then be directed into work that is productive and innovative.

2. No triangles improves decision making

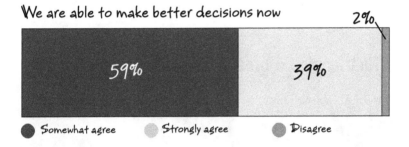

We are able to make better decisions now

59%   39%   2%

● Somewhat agree   ● Strongly agree   ● Disagree

No triangles leads to robust discussions, which in turn lead to better, more well-founded decisions.

The survey results showed 98 per cent of teams had improved decision making.

A culture of *respect trumps harmony* gives people the confidence to advance and share their ideas and experiences, and to challenge other people's assumptions. Through such candid and robust discussion a team is more likely to consider most, if not all, factors when making a decision.

No triangles also puts an end to the 'meeting after the meeting', where people who have sat through a meeting, nodding their heads and even voiced their agreement to the outcome, only to walk outside and declare, 'That won't work', and make plans to discuss the subject again at a later date.

This happens in teams where harmony is the dominant driver. People are afraid to disagree, or identify the pitfalls in an idea, in case they upset someone or are perceived as obstructive. So they sit in the meeting and go along for the ride and wait until afterwards to raise their concerns, typically in a triangle conversation.

Far better to have a culture where people separate the idea from the person: play the ball and not the man. The idea is up for discussion, and people feel free to point out potential traps or gaps in the idea. But this will only happen when there is a culture of direct conversations rather than triangles.

3. No triangles = greater innovation

Direct conversations help us to be more creative and innovative

69%   31%

● Somewhat agree   ● Strongly agree

A culture of no triangles leads to greater innovation because people offer candid ideas and feedback.

Implementing *no triangles* boosted creativity in 69 per cent of teams. The remaining 31 per cent replied that innovation wasn't a large requirement of their roles, so there was no discernible impact.

Individuals are willing to advance the crazy, untested, yet potentially game-changing ideas without fear of criticism. A culture of *no triangles* ensures people will speak up and offer the benefit of their past experience.

In a culture where harmony prevails over respect, people are reluctant to offer a different opinion or to share an experience that goes against the prevailing wisdom. They won't put their hand up and propose a conflicting idea. To keep the peace they will keep their experiences and ideas to themselves if they feel expressing them will cause conflict.

A WORD ON BRAINSTORMING

Almost all of us, at some stage in our careers, have been involved in a brainstorming session. If you've only done so a dozen or so times, you're lucky—you really have dodged a bullet!

The usual rules of brainstorming sessions are to:

1. generate as many ideas as possible
2. prioritise unusual or original ideas
3. combine and refine the ideas generated
4. abstain from criticism throughout the exercise.

The process, which should be informal and unstructured, is based on two old psychological premises: first, that the mere presence of others can have a motivating effect on an individual's performance; and, second, that quantity (eventually) leads to quality and a better outcome.

Most of us believe that two heads are better than one, and that collaborating as a group allows us to bounce ideas creatively off one another. We also presume that if you ban criticism within these groups, it will encourage greater creativity because people won't fear judgement for proposing fresh, unpolished, even crazy ideas.

Yet a recent meta-analytic review of over 800 teams showed that individuals are more likely to generate a higher number of original ideas when *not* interacting with others. People are also more likely to give up in a brainstorming session when they don't feel as though their efforts are being seriously considered or are productive.

Think back to your last brainstorming session. You may have noticed that, by and large, most of the ideas came from the more vocal, extroverted members of the team. Brainstorming tends to exclude the potential contributions of an entire population of problem-solvers who happen to be more reserved or introverted. And for those who do participate, there may still be some reluctance to fully express their ideas owing to their more reserved, introverted nature.

So why do we continue with the practice? Because even though groups don't generate more or better ideas, brainstorming is arguably more democratic than the alternatives, so it can enhance buy-in and subsequent implementation of the ideas generated, regardless of the quality of those ideas. It helps people feel like they are part of the process.

To improve brainstorming sessions, try writing down ideas instead:

- Have each participant write his or her ideas down silently.

- After the ideas have been captured, share them in round-robin fashion.

- Do multiple sessions of writing, followed by sharing, so people have a chance to build on one another's ideas.

Another way to optimise your brainstorming is to ignore the traditional limit on criticism and open up your session to a little healthy debate. Charlan Nemeth, a professor of psychology at Berkeley, found in a series of studies in 2003 that criticism can enhance the quality and quantity of viable creative ideas.

Nemeth asked a team of students to come up with solutions to a problem without criticising one another, and asked another group to brainstorm freely but also to be willing to critique one another. The team who were encouraged to challenge one another came up with 20 per cent more creative ideas than the others did.

We often fear that conflict is bad for morale, but it turns out that an environment in which dissent is encouraged can spark greater engagement with other viewpoints, and forces people to constantly re-evaluate their own ideas. Remember to lay the respectful groundwork; make sure all criticism is constructive and debates never get personal. In the right environment, where *respect trumps harmony*, opposition can lead to greater ingenuity.

4. No triangles improves accountability

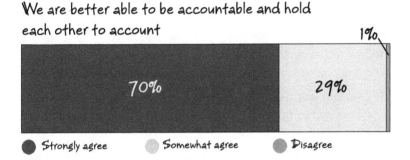

We are better able to be accountable and hold each other to account

| 70% | 29% | 1% |

● Strongly agree   ◐ Somewhat agree   ○ Disagree

A culture of no triangles improves accountability because it reduces answer shopping and ensures people go directly to the appropriate person when a decision needs to be made.

The survey results showed 99 per cent of people felt *no triangles* improved accountability, with 70 per cent of those surveyed replying they strongly agreed with the statement, 'We are better able to be accountable, and hold each other to account'. It was especially successful in stopping the 'answer shopping'.

Answer shopping behaviour commonly occurs in franchises and family businesses. As the business grows the owners find they are spending too much time in the business and not enough time *on* the business. They are too mired in detail to have the time and energy to devote to strategic planning, so they engage a manager to take over day-to-day operations. It is essential that the relationship between the manager and the owner is rock-solid, with clear accountability.

> ## Case study: Answer shopping and the franchise owner
>
> One franchisee I heard of recently was operating five retail outlets. He was in the fast-moving consumer goods (FMCG) caper, so naturally summer was a busy time for the stores.
>
> As a result, the team agreed that annual leave would not be taken in January. Everyone knew and understood this, which was fine until one of the shop assistants decided he wanted to take his annual leave in January, so he put in his request to the store manager. She turned him down, because it was by far their busiest time and being one person down would put added pressure on the rest of the team.
>
> So the shop assistant then went over her head to email the owner. The owner, unaware of the manager's decision, and believing it was a one-off situation, approved the leave request.
>
> The upshot was that the assistant got his annual leave and the manager was completely disempowered.
>
> The manager spoke to the owner, explaining the impact his overriding her decision had on her and the team, but the owner was reluctant to reverse his decision and be seen as weak and not the one in charge. Unsurprisingly, three months later the manager resigned.

5. No triangles reduces gossip

We have effectively eliminated idol gossip from our team

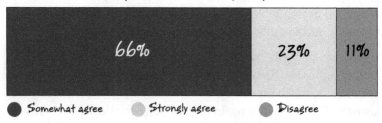

66% 23% 11%

● Somewhat agree   ● Strongly agree   ● Disagree

While it is incredibly difficult to stop gossip entirely in a workplace, it was great to see in our survey results that 66 per cent of teams who had implemented *no triangles* reported they had effectively eliminated idle gossip from their team.

Idle gossip may be less destructive in the short term than malicious gossip, but it's still something you need to deal with. Speculation, innuendo and the passing on of private information can be really harmful to relationships when that information (usually misinformation) finds its way back to the person being spoken about (and it usually does!). It erodes trust and confidence, which is the last thing you want for your team.

MENTAL HEALTH

One of the most important reasons for implementing *no triangles* and creating a culture where respect trumps harmony is the positive affect it has on mental health.

The reasons for this are twofold:

1. In a culture where harmony is the dominant driver and we're told everything is great, everything is wonderful, it becomes very difficult to put your hand up and say, 'Actually *I'm* not so great right now'. People are more likely to hide any mental health concerns they may have. They feel they need to keep up the pretense that everything is wonderful, so they remain silent about what troubles them.

2. A culture of gossip and sniping behind people's back compounds stress. Anyone feeling even remotely vulnerable will feel worse knowing they are being spoken about, often in unflattering terms, among their colleagues. A team with *no triangles* reduces this behaviour and the fear of it. It improves mental health because people understand that even though someone may not like them, they will treat them with respect and not discuss them behind their back.

MENTAL HEALTH AND NQR: AN ANTARCTIC STORY

One of the most important things we can do to reduce stress in teams, and improve mental health, is to openly discuss how we are coping.

One day in Antarctica I was feeling homesick. Now, many expats will tell you they experience bouts of homesickness, often around significant days—anniversaries, birthdays, Christmas. It was the Thursday before Good Friday (I remember it vividly!) and I was acutely missing my family.

As I was walking downstairs for breakfast Ben stopped me and asked, 'How are you going, Rach?'

How was I going? A really simple question that we generally ask people all the time.

A million thoughts raced through my head. Should I tell him I was homesick? Should I explain that while I was really enjoying the expedition and loving Antarctica, today I just missed my family and yearned to go home, just for a weekend, to give my loved ones a hug. Or would such an admission make me sound soft? Would he think this is why women shouldn't be expedition leaders, because they can't handle the long family separation?

In that split second I decided to tell him the truth.

That moment turned out to be really important for the developing culture of the team, for a couple of reasons. Firstly, it humanised me. People often think of leaders as divorced from feelings and emotions. They aren't, of course. They are just the same as everyone else. Disclosing how I was truly feeling illustrated this.

Secondly, and more importantly, it helped empower others to be open and honest about how they were feeling. When the leader shows vulnerability, it makes it okay for others to do the same. Eventually it became a common topic of conversation, and we even created our own term for it: NQR, for Not Quite Right.

To explain, NQR is the name of an Australian discount supermarket that sells heavily reduced groceries, and some of the items may have a damaged label or discoloured printing. They are perfectly fine to consume, but they can look a tad ... NQR.

So NQR became our shorthand. When someone asked how you were going, instead of saying, 'I'm okay. I'm just a bit homesick right now and wish I could go home and see the family for a day or two', you could simply say, 'Oh, you know, I'm just a bit NQR'.

This shorthand was vitally important because it built empathy and eliminated bravado. If you told someone you were feeling a bit NQR you knew they understood what you meant—they got it. There was no judgement, no surprise, just a bucketload of empathy and understanding.

It also put an end to the nonsense of the false bravado around 'We're tough Antarctic expeditioners—we don't get homesick'. Of course we did. Many of our team were parents, some with very young children. We didn't have Skype or Facetime (because of bandwidth limitations) so the parents missed out on their children for an entire year. They got to speak to them on the phone, but they didn't see their beautiful faces. Of course they missed them and of course they got homesick.

The ability to speak openly about this without fear of judgement was so important.

6. No triangles builds respect

No Triangles has helped us respect each others differences

58%   42%

● Strongly agree   ● Somewhat agree

No triangles builds greater respect in a team, so we better appreciate one another's differences.

Every single person surveyed responded that a culture of *no triangles* built respect. The evidence is unequivocal. Take off the table the idea that we all need to love each other and get along, and replace it with the resolution that we treat each other with respect, and people are more willing to accept differences.

The challenge is to go beyond tolerance and to recognise and respect that we're different from each other. As a team we are the sum of a vast array of different parts, with each person bringing different experiences, skills, beliefs and knowledge to the team. That difference is a competitive advantage—once you know how to harness it.

Case study: Emperor penguins and collaboration

The Emperor penguin is the only living animal in Antarctica during the winter after all the whales, seals and other birds have moved north (well, except for us, and we have a lot of technological and practical help). The only way they survive is through teamwork. They huddle together in a tight group, with every bird taking its turn on the outside of the huddle, bracing against the freezing winds and temperatures that reach an extreme of 30 degrees celcius below zero. When they have had enough they move into the middle, and the birds in the middle move to the outside. In this way they rotate so every

---

bird has a turn on the outside and every bird has time in the warmer, more protected centre.

They have adapted this extraordinary behaviour as a survival mechanism. Every other bird species on the planet has a nest, or a patch or a turf to protect. But the Emperor penguins recognise that if they were each to protect their individual patch they simply would not survive the Antarctic winter. Their recognition that their very survival depends on protecting the whole 'tribe' offers a fantastic metaphor for any team. Keep the team strong, resilient and relevant and every member of it can thrive.

I often wonder about how all it would take would be for one bird, just one single bird, to say, 'I'm not going to the outside today. It's too cold'. Just one bird. Then another bird would think, 'Well, if he's not doing it, I'm not either', and before long the whole system would collapse.

(Note: I say 'he' because these are the male penguins. The females go to sea to feed for exactly 63 days. Or, for all I know, they're just sitting around a headland drinking Pina Coladas and watching Netflix.)

It takes only one individual to show disrespect to undermine the whole team.

7. No triangles improves feedback

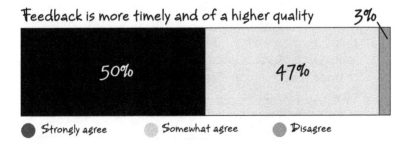

Feedback is more timely and of a higher quality in a culture where respect trumps harmony.

From our interviews with the 200 teams who have implemented *no triangles*, we know that, on average, it takes about two months to embed the behaviour in the culture. It requires consistency and constant reminders before it becomes just 'how we do things around here'.

The good news is it's worth it, with 97 per cent of those surveyed saying it improved feedback. Once the culture becomes one of respect over harmony, people give feedback more readily. We learn to use facts and confirmed data and to separate the behaviour from the person, so people are much less likely to take offence.

In any conversations, the three most important factors for giving feedback are:

1. **Timing and timeliness.** Choose the right time and place. Don't hold the conversation when the other party is upset or angry. Respect the other person's privacy by minimising the chances of you being overheard. As soon as you realise you need to have this conversation, do it! Don't dwell on it; leaving it too long only makes it more difficult. Also, whenever possible, have these conversations face-to-face.

2. **Using facts and data.** Turn on your LADAR (Language Radar) and listen for *ping* words such as *always, never, everyone, no one, can't, won't*. Avoid saying things like, 'Everyone in the department feels the same way' or 'I've heard this from countless people'. Often when we hear these kinds of statements, we automatically discount them, because we know in most cases they are, at best, exaggerations. If the issue is so serious that you need to bring others into the discussion, make sure they are present. Listen to both yourself and the other person. If you exaggerate, quickly clarify. If they do, ask for specifics. Rely on facts.

3. **Following up.** Consolidate and move forward. Try to speak to the person again within a day or two, even if on

an entirely unrelated matter. It keeps the conversation in perspective and conveys that you said what you had to say and are now prepared to move on.

8. No triangles = positive morale

Implementing No Triangles has had a positive effect on morale

| 54% | 46% |

● Strongly agree   ● Somewhat agree

For me, the most startling and positive result from this research was the fact every single respondent reported that implementing *no triangles* improved morale. Of the 200 teams who are using *no triangles* as a teamwork tool every person agreed it had improved morale, with over half (54 per cent) saying they strongly agreed.

Feeling valued and recognised for the work you do is the bedrock of employee morale. The Randstad World of Work survey reported that '38 per cent of respondents said being valued and recognised was their top motivator, followed by a strong understanding of how their role contributes to achieving organisational goals. Salary and remuneration were not as highly valued.'

In Antarctica I spent considerable time ensuring that every person understood in some detail the tasks performed by every other member of the community. It started as a simple social event entitled 'A Day in the Life...' at which we shared a cake (scientists) or a barbecue (plumbers) or afternoon tea (doctor), and the host showed us the tasks they completed on an average day. This simple social ceremony turned into something vastly more important as each person came to understand, and value, the contribution of his or her peers. The question 'What do they do all day?' was asked and answered.

In the quest to retain talent in a highly mobile workforce, this value and recognition becomes even more important. It was especially notable in the world of IT and telecommunications, where employees responded in higher numbers than other industries, that value and recognition (31 per cent) and understanding how their role fitted into the organisation (24 per cent) were their biggest motivators.

A culture of *no triangles* has a significant impact on morale (100 per cent of respondents agreed on this!) because you know the rest of the team is on your side. They may not love you or even much like you, but they respect you, and you know that if they have something to say about you, then you'll hear it from them first, not from a third party. How reassuring is that?

Quantifying no triangles: where are the savings?

According to Safe Work Australia, 6 per cent of all serious workers compensation claims are for work-related mental health conditions. A number of subcategories contribute to this figure including (but not limited to):

- work load and workplace
- work schedule
- organisational culture and function
- interpersonal relationships at work.

Interpersonal relationships can include issues such as social or physical isolation, poor relations with supervisors and managers, interpersonal conflict, and bullying and harassment.

The impact of mental stress on an organisation can be considerable. In 2012–13 Safe Work Australia reported that mental stress claims cost the Australian economy approximately

$3 billion, accounting for 5 per cent of the total economic cost of work-related injuries and illness ($61 billion). This equates to approximately $292 000 per case.

However, there are additional costs associated with mental health conditions and compensation claims, including restaffing, retraining, high staff turnover and lengthy periods of absence.

No triangles and *respect trumps harmony* can have a positive influence in a number of these areas, as they provide frameworks that give people the confidence to raise issues at the earliest possible time, thereby preventing unnecessary hurt and potential escalation. They are strategies that can be implemented at both an organisational and an individual level, and if supported at senior levels, they demonstrate a commitment to open and transparent communication across the workforce.

A number of organisations that have implemented *no triangles* have seen an improvement in their culture and have made a direct correlation to the strategy. They have further identified a significant increase in staff confidence and resilience:

'The benefits of *no triangles* have been an increase in confidence from staff to manage the issue themselves, to talk directly to one another and to work out how to help each other.'

'One staff member who had felt bullied now feels much better as a result of being able to have more direct conversations.'

'*No triangles* has definitely had a positive impact as it has helped to build resilience and confidence in people to have constructive conversations.'

No triangles in schools

Governments have recently renewed efforts to address gender-based violence in schools through what is now referred to as respectful relationships education.

This kind of education is included in the Australian Curriculum, but not all state and territory governments have been proactive in making it mandatory. Victoria's 2016 Royal Commission into Family Violence recommended respectful relationships education be made mandatory in every school from prep to Year 12. The program is now being implemented in more than 1000 government, Catholic and independent schools in Victoria.

Respectful relationships education seeks to prevent violence before it occurs. This is fostered through supporting schools to challenge and find alternatives to the rigid gender roles that underpin gender inequality and lead to violence against women.

While the focus here is on gender and violence, my research shows that *no triangles* can complement a respectful relationships program by providing a practical tool to help build respect.

Schools that have implemented *no triangles* have reported its benefits:

> 'I use the strategy with students and staff as well as parents, because I want to encourage people to have the conversation directly and early.'

> 'I want to be able to provide students with tools they can use when communicating and managing relationships.'

> 'I'm using it with my students (13- to 18-year-olds), and I'm finding that they are more confident and want to be respectful.'

One respondent, a head of department with 22 staff, noted, 'Sometimes people can be worked up about a situation. In these circumstances I tell them to wait and be ready and calm before they have the conversation so they don't unintentionally escalate matters. I've had no direct feedback but I'm aware that unless there's a major problem, people are generally able to deal with the issue themselves, which has freed up my time and energy.'

Her next challenge, she reported, was to provide more training on active listening and coaching people about not becoming defensive. 'It's also about how the message is delivered', she added.

A real-life case study put to the test

Poor communication in the workplace can lead to significant problems, including conflict, low employee morale, lack of team cohesion, reduced productivity and, in some cases, injury to employees.

Quite often, however, the breakdown in communication may simply be a misunderstanding of another person's expectations. Early and direct conversations can prevent these problems from occurring and build stronger and more effective teams.

Feelings of uncertainty and doubt can lead to a lack of confidence, increased stress and the development of poor team culture including gossip, resentment and low productivity. The following example traces the results of one case of under-communication.

THE SITUATION

When a new manager was appointed to the team 12 months ago, he immediately began a restructure of the team, which resulted in significant changes to several roles. One employee in particular felt there had been insufficient consultation regarding the restructure and she was now experiencing a lack of role clarity.

The manager was aware of the employee's concerns and had several discussions with her to attempt to provide the clarity needed and ensure support was available, but the employee remained upset about the situation.

THE ESCALATION

Over a period of time, the employee became increasingly disengaged from her work, refusing to undertake tasks given to her that she felt were not part of her role. She also began to share her criticisms of the situation and of the manager with other members of the team. By this point she was failing to show common courtesies by not discussing her concerns directly with the manager, failing to provide help on request, refusing to complete work and constantly disparaging the manager in conversations with other staff.

Finally the manager set up a meeting with the employee to discuss her performance, but they were unable to work through the issues as the employee became so upset that the meeting had to be cut short.

THE IMPACT

The employee had become so anxious and emotional about the situation that she consulted with her doctor and was certified unfit to return to work. During this week off she continued to discuss her perceived treatment by the manager with other team members.

Shortly after this, a second employee who had been involved in the conversations began to disengage, also complaining of insufficient support and communication. This employee did not raise her concerns directly with the manager until a performance discussion was convened. Following this meeting the employee consulted with her doctor and was also certified unfit for work.

The remaining team members were put under significant workload and time pressures as the tasks assigned to the two employees were reassigned among them. Effectiveness and productivity within the team were significantly undermined.

By now the manager himself also began to experience significant stress and anxiety in his efforts to manage the workload across the team and within his budget, while managing the two return-to-work situations, and the impact of the allegations made by the employees despite his efforts to provide guidance and support.

THE OUTCOME

The first employee's perception of the manager, driven in part by his management style and the changes to her role, meant she felt unable to have the necessary conversation about what she needed from him to perform her new tasks so she could not understand how she fit into the team. This was complicated by the fact that she attributed the problem to the manager's lack of ability, which she openly discussed with other members of the team. The result of this was constant gossip, low morale and disengagement within the team.

While the manager had provided information and support to the employee and the rest of the team, he considered that, given her level, she should have been able to take some initiative and use her judgement regarding tasks and priorities. The manager did not have this conversation with the employee and did not intervene in the gossip and inappropriate conversations. This resulted in the situation escalating to a performance discussion, which increased the stress and anxiety on the employee.

Both employees remained unfit for work for several months, with the initial employee being deemed unable to return to the team indefinitely.

Because of budget restraints the manager was unable to backfill the positions, which resulted in an increasing amount of stress for the remainder of the team.

Why early and direct communication is needed

This real-life case highlights the need for good communication and management of a situation at the earliest opportunity. Both the manager and the employee needed to be clear regarding their expectations and what they needed from each other in their respective roles.

The obvious consequences of this lack of communication were:

- two staff members with medically diagnosed mental health conditions
- additional pressure and stress placed on the manager and team through an increased workload
- a culture of uncertainty and rumour
- a drop in productivity and effectiveness.

Unseen consequences included:

- significant additional resources, including the HR and employee relations team, required to support the process and those employees involved

- significant unplanned leave
- potential compensation claims.

Exceptions to the no triangles rule

No triangles is a practical and proven tool for strengthening teamwork. But it is also simply a rule of thumb for behaviour, a commitment. As in most areas of life, there are of course exceptions to the rule.

Here I'll identify four exceptions, although there are certainly more:

1. **Safety and risk.** It is absolutely fine to escalate a safety issue or take it to a third party if you have any concerns. Similarly, if you identify a risk that will damage the reputation of the business, by all means consult another person.

2. **Mental health.** If you have any concerns at all about a person's mental health, it is important to discuss these with them; if you are still concerned, then talk to HR or phone your Employee Assistance Program or Peer Support team for advice.

3. **Bullying and harassment.** If you notice someone is being bullied or harassed, or someone reveals to you that they are being bullied or harassed at work, then ask them if they would like your support in raising the issue with management. If they agree to it, then there is nothing wrong with your raising the issue with the appropriate manager yourself.

4. **Tried and didn't work.** If you have tried the *no triangles* approach and have spoken to someone directly to try to sort out an issue, but the issue remains unresolved, or the person disagrees with your take on the situation, then by all means involve your line manager. You can't keep trying the same thing to get the same result. Escalate it.

FINAL THOUGHTS

The results are in: a focus on respect over harmony improves everything from team morale to productivity. It increases innovation and promotes candid discussions, which leads to better decision making.

How do you know if you have the balance between respect and harmony wrong and you're placing too much emphasis on keeping the peace?

1. Teams fail to make difficult trade-offs when prioritising work, which leads to overwhelming workloads. A fear of saying 'no' means the list simply grows.

2. Leaders tolerate poor performance and dysfunctional behaviour, which means other employees have to pick up the slack. Or they create a work-around so others don't have to deal with the problem person.

3. *Bacon wars* will flourish and fester when people don't feel it's safe to express dissent or frustration, so resentment continues to build.

In an era in which high stress and mental illness are so prevalent, and increasing, it's essential to create environments where people feel they can speak up and resolve issues in a professional and timely manner before they develop into major crises.

By changing priorities so respect is the goal, rather than a desire for everyone to get along, we provide multiple opportunities to create, to solve, to innovate and to support one another. We accept that people are different, and we step beyond tolerance and actually respect that difference. And maybe, just maybe, with all this shared respect we can make the world a better place. Because *respect trumps harmony*, every time.

APPENDIX I

Frequently asked questions about no triangles

I've tried without success to implement *no triangles*. What now?

Our survey results, plus years of anecdotal evidence, show that the number one reason for a lack of success with introducing *no triangles* to a team is a misunderstanding about driving cultural change. It's difficult to achieve and requires clarity and consistency.

You need to be clear about why you are implementing the concept (*clarity*).

You also need to apply the same rules to everyone (*consistency*). Keep calling out the behaviour and point out the obvious: if you don't talk to him and I won't … what's going to change?

If the triangle concerned is triggered by answer shopping—that is, someone going over your head to get what they want—then follow up with them and explain the impact that has on you and the team, and how it promotes a culture of disrespect.

Implementation requires a full commitment from the team, so the best place to start is a team planning day or a team meeting where *everyone* is in attendance. The team needs to agree on what triangles look like for them, and what to do about them.

Why do people initiate triangles?

There are many reasons. Sometimes it's simply to share their discomfort or frustration. Often it's to garner support so they can claim that it's not just their own point of view, but rather that 'everyone else agrees with me'.

But in reality it is rarely *everyone*.

People have told me it's to sound out whether their reaction is proportionate, to validate what they are feeling. Which is fine if you are talking about the issue concerned, and you confine the conversation to the facts and how you feel. Don't personalise and interpret someone else's intent to boost your case.

We judge ourselves on our intent, but we judge others on their impact. Some people use triangles to influence an outcome — they go over a manager's head to get the result they want.

Why do people enable triangles to continue?

Usually because it's easier. Having the triangle conversation removes the distraction in the short term so people have their say and can get back to work.

We can often perceive it as no big deal. I'm just venting, letting off steam! No harm no foul! That is, until the other person finds out we've been complaining about them. And if you have complained to the boss then you've also escalated and elevated the issue, so now your target will be even more angry. Your first point of contact should always be with the person concerned. How they choose to respond is their prerogative, but you have done the respectful thing by coming to them directly.

Some leaders allow triangles to flourish because of a misguided notion of leadership. I did this myself for many years, believing it was my job as leader to listen to all my people's frustrations and angst so they could get on with their work. I also mistakenly believed I wasn't contributing to the problem by simply listening, when in fact my behaviour sent a clear message that complaining about someone behind their back was totally acceptable.

For some leaders it makes them feel needed and powerful. Information is power. A person caught up in a myriad triangles may have access to a huge amount of personal information about who gets along with who, and who doesn't, who is perceived as competent and who isn't, and all the other dynamics of office politics. Informational power is derived from a person's ability to control the information that others need to accomplish something. Often the information is simply idle gossip and untrue, which is why a culture of *no triangles* is so important for building respect.

How do I set the tone if I'm in management?

When you put respect ahead of harmony, you are delivering the following messages about your principles as a leader:

- I will do what's necessary to lead and develop a high-performance team.
- I care enough about you as a professional to be honest with you.
- I care enough about you as a person to deliver this honesty in a way that leaves you feeling respected, but clear about how effectively you are doing your job.
- I care enough about the team to immediately call out the behaviour of any team member who is undermining the cultural standards we have agreed on.
- In my absence I expect all team members to hold each other to the same high standards.

What if you're in a toxic culture?

If you are working in a toxic environment and don't feel you can leave right now, here are two tips for keeping sane and productive:

1. **Hold on to your personal boundaries.** Don't get caught up in what others are doing. You can't change or manage them, but you can change and manage your own reactions. Make sure the things you're doing fit with your values and you aren't just going with the flow. Keep your distance from activities you don't respect unless you feel your voice can make a difference. Implement *no triangles* just for yourself. If someone approaches you and wants to gossip or complain about another person, tell them you're trying to practise *no triangles* so you'd rather not listen. It's like a diet—don't tempt me!

2. **Focus on solutions, not problems.** Even when it's obvious or justified, complaining and grumbling just contributes to the spread of toxicity. Whether it's aimed at other employees, company leadership or specific policies, complaining feeds a mentality of defeat and breeds exhaustion. When others are focused on the problems, devote your own energy to focusing on solutions. It will change up the conversation, and eventually it may even change the culture.

What if your social culture frowns on conflict and thinks harmony is more important?

I've worked extensively across Asia, and in many countries there is a priority on keeping the peace, saving face and generally supporting a harmonious environment. Many cultures also value hierarchy over initiative.

It becomes problematic when you are working for a multinational company and there is an expectation that you will show leadership, irrespective of your title or position in the hierarchy. The tension between the two is significant and complex.

But at some stage you will need to have a difficult conversation. In these cultures, one easy tool to use is to paraphrase. Instead of directly giving facts and data to someone in a confronting manner, ask questions, such as 'My understanding of the situation is x. Is that how you see it?' or 'So what I hear you say is …' or 'What I think you are telling me is …' or 'Have I got this right? Is that a fair description of the situation?' It is a much gentler, less aggressive way of holding the conversation.

Is there a difference between genders and between generations?

While my research didn't capture age or gender information, I know anecdotally, from presenting on this topic over 15 years, that there are noticeable differences between genders and generations.

Specifically, in female-dominated industries—teaching, nursing, childcare—the issue of triangle conversations is much greater. I ascribe this to the age-old notion that traditionally women were raised to believe that 'if you have nothing nice to say, then don't say anything at all'. Thus, some women become conflict averse after years of little experience in dealing with conflict.

Men are more often raised to be leaders, to speak up, to stand up for themselves. Generally, they have had much more experience dealing with conflict and difficult conversations.

Similarly, older generations more often tend to keep silent and bite their tongue, rather than rock the boat. I put this down to younger generations growing up with social media. Gen Y and the Millennials have always had social media, so they have always been in a position to offer an opinion, which means they are more comfortable saying what they think. But more importantly, they are ready to receive feedback more often, even if it's not positive feedback. They genuinely want to know how they are performing at work and in volunteer roles because they have grown up with constant and instant feedback through likes and comments on social media.

APPENDIX II

10 steps for difficult conversations

No triangles only works when you have the process and culture to support it. The following process was developed to support my people when they knew they had to have a difficult conversation with someone. It's not exhaustive or comprehensive, but it's a useful guide that can signpost the way to prepare, conduct and conclude a difficult conversation.

Before — planning what to say and when to say it

1. **Timing and timeliness.** Choose the right time and place and as soon as you realise you need to have a conversation, do it! Don't dwell on it. Leaving it too long only makes it more difficult. Trust me, you won't want to 'sleep on it'.

2. **Anticipate that you may not be on the same page.** Different perceptions of intent, interpretations of the facts, and judgement about what is right or best are usually at the root of all difficult conversations.

3. **Rehearse**. If time permits it is helpful to capture the details of the situation in writing. Include what you wish both parties to achieve. This gives you an opportunity to consider all views and nuances of the situation. Taking the time to properly prepare for any important conversation yields better results.

During — keeping the conversation on track

4. **What and why.** Use specific examples. What is at stake? Why does this matter? Rely on facts to take the heat out of the situation — for example, the fact is you didn't meet the deadline for this project. Mind your language — avoid words like *no one, everyone, always* and *never*.

5. **Identify your role in the problem.** How have you contributed to the situation? For example, 'By not bringing this to your attention earlier I added to the growing rift between you and the others'.

6. **Maintain eye contact.** As in any constructive face-to-face communication, maintaining eye contact helps you gauge the receptivity of the other person throughout the conversation and demonstrates your honesty and desire to listen to them closely.

7. **Stay in control.** If you express anger, it is natural for the other person to match your emotional state. Do whatever it takes to remain calm and cool. Silence, pausing and even inserting an 'okay' here and there are all effective in keeping the conversation calm and measured.

8. **Don't interrupt.** Never interrupt when the other person is speaking. Show them the respect you want them to show you. Don't look like you are anxious to respond. People who can't wait to speak generally aren't listening because they are so focused on their own arguments.

9. **Don't team up**. Avoid saying things like, 'Everyone in the department feels the same way' or 'I have heard about

this from countless people'. When we hear these kinds of absolute statements, we tend to discount what is being said because in most cases they are exaggerations at best.

If there is an issue that needs to be addressed, resist the temptation to strengthen your position by including others. If the issue is so serious that you need to bring others into the discussion, make sure they are present.

Afterwards — consolidating and moving forward

10. **Follow up.** Try to speak to the person again in a day or two, even on an entirely unrelated matter. It keeps the conversation in perspective and shows you said what you needed to say and are now prepared to move on.

INDEX